THE EAST-WEST CENTER—officially known as the Center for Cultural and Technical Interchange Between East and West—is a national educational institution established in Hawaii by the United States Congress in 1960 to promote better relations and understanding between the United States and the nations of Asia and the Pacific through cooperative study, training, and research. The Center is administered by a public, nonprofit corporation whose international Board of Governors consists of distinguished scholars, business leaders, and public servants.

Each year more than 1,500 men and women from many nations and cultures participate in Center programs that seek cooperative solutions to problems of mutual consequence to East and West. Working with the Center's multidisciplinary and multicultural staff, participants include visiting scholars and researchers; leaders and professionals from the academic, government, and business communities; and graduate degree students, most of whom are enrolled at the University of Hawaii. For each Center participant from the United States, two participants are sought from the Asian and Pacific area.

Center programs are conducted by institutes addressing problems of communication, culture learning, environment and policy, population, and resource systems. A limited number of "open" grants are available to degree scholars and research fellows whose academic interests are not encompassed by institute programs.

The United States Congress provides basic funding for Center programs and a variety of awards to participants. Because of the cooperative nature of Center programs, financial support and cost-sharing are also provided by Asian and Pacific governments, regional agencies, private enterprise and foundations. The Center is on land adjacent to and provided by the University of Hawaii.

East-West Center Books are published by The University Press of Hawaii to further the Center's aims and programs.

THE EAST-WEST CULTURE LEARNING INSTITUTE is one of five "problem-oriented" institutes at the East-West Center. The central concern of the Institute is that special set of problems of understanding that arise among peoples of the United States, Asia, and the Pacific when they interact cross-culturally. The objective of the Institute is to investigate the nature of cross-national interaction and to suggest ways of solving or dealing with the problems of understanding that accompany it.

Verner C. Bickley, Director
Editorial Board
    J. G. Amirthanayagam
    Jerry Boucher
    William Feltz
    Mark P. Lester, Chairman
    Robert Snow

The Place
of Literature
in the Teaching
of English
as a Second
or Foreign Language

The Place of Literature in the Teaching of English as a Second or Foreign Language

ALBERT H. MARCKWARDT

Ⓔ AN EAST-WEST CENTER BOOK
FROM THE EAST-WEST CULTURE LEARNING INSTITUTE
Published for the East-West Center
by The University Press of Hawaii

Library of Congress Cataloging in Publication Data

Marckwardt, Albert Henry, 1903–1975
   The place of literature in the teaching of
English as a second or foreign language.

   Bibliography: p.
   1. English language—Study and teaching—
Foreign students. 2. Literature—Study and
teaching. I. Title.
PE1128.A2M34   420'.7   77–25360
ISBN 0–8248–0606–9

Contents

Foreword

I AM GRATEFUL to have been given the sad privilege of introducing Albert H. Marckwardt's last book. In many ways it is an epitome of his life's work, representing as it does his love of English studies as a whole, his refusal as a linguist to regard literature as anything but central to his concerns, his deep interest in the teaching of English in every part of the world. Its value as a bequest, moreover, lies in its author's well-nigh uniquely wide and long experience as a teacher and an adviser of teachers and in the succinct way in which it presents the fruits of this experience.

Written in "retirement," when Professor Marckwardt was working with unremitting and characteristic energy at—with symbolic appropriateness—the East-West Center, Hawaii, the book reflects a mind not merely well-informed on the most controversial issues of teaching English as a second and as a foreign language but boldly determined to tackle them. He has left us much to argue over: specialists will fruitfully debate several of his detailed analyses, prognoses, and prescriptions. But few will fail to be convinced by the main lines of his book—a twofold thesis which in both respects is strictly congruent with his persuasively argued approach on related issues over the years.

First, despite the varied aims and conditions of English teaching, Professor Marckwardt argues unequivocally that literature has an indispensable place in the curriculum. But this is in no way to bolster up the old élitist attitudes of English teachers intent on transmitting their own expertise in the metaphysicals or Pope, still less to ignore recent demands for "relevance."

FOREWORD

Second, just as he always insisted on seeing English as overwhelmingly a single language, so he viewed it as essential to regard all literature in English as significantly and fundamentally a single literature—the cultural product "of a world-wide linguistic and intellectual commonwealth."

All in all, precisely the kind of last word that Professor Marckwardt would have wished to leave with us.

RANDOLPH QUIRK

University College London

The Place
of Literature
in the Teaching
of English
as a Second
or Foreign Language

CHAPTER 1
Issues
and Assumptions

FOR MANY YEARS, and indeed until quite recently, the reading of literature was regarded as the capstone of the foreign-language learning experience. This was true, at least, of the Western World. The student of German climaxed his studies with a course in Faust, his Spanish counterpart
with the reading of Cervantes and the works of the *Siglo del Oro*. When
English was studied as a foreign language, all roads led to Shakespeare.

The reason for this would seem to be fairly clear. From the time of the
Renaissance until the middle of the nineteenth century, the two foreign
languages which held undisputed sway in the classroom were Latin and
ancient Greek. Except for the liturgical use of the former, there would
have been little reason for studying those languages as current media of
communication; certainly not after the seventeenth-century decline of
the use of Latin as the language of science and of international diplomacy. If a mastery of them was to be put to any use at all, it would have
to be primarily a reading knowledge. The materials to be read consisted
of the works of the ancient philosophers, historians, poets, and drama-
tists. And, in fact, this is still the situation as it applies to the study of
Latin and ancient Greek today.

Shortly after the middle of the nineteenth century, the modern
Western languages began to encroach upon the place of the ancient
languages in the curriculum. Their advocates made the case for them
primarily on the grounds of practical utility. They were living, not dead
languages. Important scientific works were written in them. Each of
them possessed a literature broad in extent, high in quality. On the basis
of such arguments, an acquaintance with the literature remained as an

important factor, but it was no longer the primary motive for study. This was especially true in the United States, a country always notable for its pragmatic approach to education.

The mid-twentieth century brought in its wake a vastly greater opportunity for the practical use of foreign languages. The dissemination, across national boundaries, of the printed word increased, and that of the spoken language even more dramatically. Air travel placed speakers of different languages into contact with each other on an unprecedented scale. In many countries the amount of time devoted to the study of foreign languages in the schools did not increase proportionately to the demands for heightened skill in their use. This has resulted in a reassessment of the aims of foreign-language study and a reconsideration of the content of the curriculum, including that of English where it is studied as a foreign or second language.

As a consequence of this reassessment, there have developed sharply divergent points of view about the place of literature in the foreign-language or second-language course. An emphatic negative reaction is to be found in an article by Professor Charles Blatchford of the Department of English as a Second Language at the University of Hawaii (1972). His conclusion, that "the study of English literature is a luxury that cannot be indulged during the limited amount of time allocated to English," is based primarily upon three considerations. He feels, first of all, that as far as the Asian nations are concerned, their primary interest is in the attainment of a functional command of the language to the point that the student will be able to handle simple English language situations involving the four skills. "With such objectives," he argues, "it follows that the classroom emphasis should be on a functional use of the language, not on literature" (p. 6).

Blatchford cites as a further objection the inadequate preparation of teachers for the task of dealing with literature in the foreign-language classroom. To substantiate his point he asserts that few ESOL training programs in the United States include literature as a requirement. In fact, only three M.A. curricula for such teachers value literature sufficiently to list specific courses in the subject that the trainees may take. The reader is also given to understand that the resources available for teacher training in Asia are meager with respect to literary content, and that the growing body of information about teaching language which the prospective teacher must master can easily fill his course of study.

Finally Blatchford contends that the current trend in the English language curriculum is toward understanding the place of language in society and its relation to the culture of a people. "The discussion of cultural understanding as a trend in ESOL can be connected with the current emphasis in the United States on bilingualism and biculturalism. The 'Guidelines' for teacher training being considered by TESOL for teachers in America place more emphasis upon an understanding of the differences in register and sociolinguistic and sociocultural understanding that a teacher must have, rather than upon literature which does not contribute to the student's ability to function in the society" (p. 7).

In all justice to Professor Blatchford, it should be pointed out that his concern is primarily with the inclusion of literature in elementary and secondary school programs, and that he does concede that "there may be more justification for literary studies where English is a second rather than a foreign language." Nevertheless, his concluding statement leaves little room for question or compromise: "The three considerations, then, of aims and objectives of English, teaching training, and trends in ESOL appear to be fairly strong reasons for not encouraging an inquiry into literature during a pupil's limited exposure to English."

The same issue of the *Culture and Language Learning Newsletter* in which Professor Blatchford's article appears also carries a discussion by Dr. Thelma Kintanar, Research Associate at the Culture Learning Institute of the East-West Center, on "The Role of Literature in Culture Learning" (1972). Although she does not deal as directly with educational or curricular issues as Professor Blatchford, she does see linguistic and literary studies touching at various points. Possibly the statement which best summarizes her view of this relationship is the following (p. 3):

> An important focus of culture learning is the learning of languages not only because language is an important part of culture and an indispensable tool of culture learning but because language learning provides analogies to culture learning. Literary study too is primarily concerned with language but with the particular uses of language in literature including, and perhaps most specially, its non-discursive and non-referential uses. Its emphasis is on the metaphorical, stylistic and other aesthetic uses of language. The linguistic interest of culture learning is broader, its approach more scientific and pragmatic, but there is no reason why it should not include in its scope the literary uses of language.

She then goes on to describe the connections between language and literature in somewhat more specific terms:

> From the point of view of the study of language and culture, literary study can make a valuable contribution in tracing the development of a language . . . as reflected in its writings; it can influence and, in fact, has influenced such development—the history of any language would be quite different without its poets and major writers. A thorough study of the development of a language, therefore, entails a study of its literature. (p. 3)

It is quite true, of course, that the issues of the place of literature in language instruction are not squarely joined in these two articles. In contrast to the very practical educational questions with which Professor Blatchford is concerned, Dr. Kintanar is interested primarily in the development of man's awareness of his culture. She takes pains to demonstrate that no matter whether one proceeds from an Arnoldian or an anthropological concept of culture, literature, by expressing both universal human values and the values of the culture out of which it has come, makes a notable and unique contribution to man's understanding of himself and his relations to other men.

A third analysis of the current disagreement over the place of literature in the curriculum is offered by Professor Peter D. Strevens (1974), who places the matter in a historical context. He begins by emphasizing the recent mushrooming rise of the demand for English for special purposes, that is to say, English to meet the needs of scientists, engineers, lawyers, and other people with very special though somewhat limited linguistic requirements. He sees this as important for the following reason:

> In our profession, up till twenty years ago, there really was only one educational framework, one set of pedagogical aims and these were considered sufficient to justify the entire profession in which we worked and that was the aims of teaching English—and this applied to all other languages as well—teaching languages, teaching English, as a part of a general education—not only, however, a general education but, indeed, a general *humanities* education. The teaching of English was automatically assumed to be part of a general education on the humanities, the arts side, with the tacit assumption that the very best students would go forward and study English literature. And this was taken for granted, this was how we operated: virtually the entire organisation and arrangements of our profession were based on this assumption. (p. 3)

He goes on to say that the situation described in the foregoing statement prevailed until about twenty years ago, at which time a new demand for English developed, "a demand this time for English unrelated to literary studies and not necessarily within the framework—indeed, outside the framework—of general education." It was a demand for English as a practical communication skill or set of skills, "made stronger in the wake of the large number of countries, particularly in Africa, also in the Indian sub-continent, which had formerly been British colonies or possessions and which were now independent and which . . . agreed that they needed to continue English as an important and probably an official language for their countries, nevertheless felt that the time was past when they needed to be linked directly with the culture, the direct, domestic day-to-day culture, of either Britain, or similarly if the culture was American, with [the] United States" (pp. 3–4).

As a result of this development, "there grew up two different kinds of learners, two different kinds of demands that learners were making upon the teachers of English. One was a continuation of the demand for English as a general educational subject linked very much to English-speaking culture . . . and the other, very much linked to the new idea that English was a communication skill needed by some of the newly-independent countries in order to further their futures and to have a window on world culture, a window on science, a window on the transnational industries of the arts, entertainment, science and so on" (p. 4).

To complicate the matter still further, Strevens sees the even more recent demand for English for Special Purposes as a third framework—"namely, of people who are looking for English but who are looking for it neither as a general educational subject limited to literature, nor as a complete command of the language skill for practical communication, but rather to do a specific job." He concludes, "Indeed, if you wanted to, you could nowadays regard literature and the study of literature as being yet another way in which English for special purposes is being supplied." This amounts, of course, to a restriction or a narrowing of the place of literature in the study of English as a foreign or second language, but it is not a call for its elimination nor is it a continuation of the tendency to see literature as the *summum bonum* of the language-learning experience.

Even somewhat earlier, the question of the place of literature had been raised by W. R. Lee in an editorial in the journal *English Language Teaching* (1970). He begins by asking the by-now familiar question:

> To what extent need learners of a foreign language study the literature?
> . . . Often the answer given is "Not at all." But what is missed, and how is the language-learning affected, if the literature is ignored?
>
> Much of the world's business is conducted in English, an international means of everyday communication. Much of science and technology is accessible in English but not in the student's own tongue. Thus the exclusion of literature from courses in English is easy to justify on vocational grounds: "We need only a means of reading and discussing science." "We need only a medium in which to conduct trade," and so on. In parts of the world where languages are many and various, English is also the means of general education for all.
>
> The substance of the English language, however, has been shaped by literature. It is in literature that the resources of the language are most fully and most skilfully used. It seems to follow that literature should enter into the

language-study of those who are to use the language with the greatest possible skill and effect.

The inclusion of literature in a language-course is also, of course, justifiable on other grounds. They are the grounds on which the study of literature is to be justified at all, in any language; and study of a foreign literature, at least where the cultural and historical tradition is on the whole the same as the learner's, may be a broadening-out of study of literature of the mother tongue.

Yet "study" seems hardly the word, summoning-up as it does the image of the mature student bent over his books. Lyrics are to be heard and not merely seen, plays are to be seen and heard. Literature is rooted, so far as the foreign-language learner is concerned, in the oral basis of language learning; rooted in lively and meaningful oral drills, in spoken and acted dialogues, in simple dramatisation of stories; indeed in those very procedures which make for successful and interested learning of the language.

The printed literature cannot come to life if this basis has been lacking: it will remain largely impenetrable on the page if the reader is deaf, in the ear of imagination and memory, to its sound. Reading one's own literature one is never incapacitated by such deafness.

The question of the place of literature in the experience of the language learner is by no means confined to the teaching of English. It has been a moot point in the teaching of foreign languages in the United States. Over the past twenty years, ten working committees of the Northeast Conference on the Teaching of Foreign Languages have considered the matter, and in the interval between 1954 and 1967, eleven separate reports were issued. In addition, there has been much discussion of the subject in the journals of the so-called AAT organizations, that is to say in *Hispania*, the organ of the American Association of Teachers of Spanish and Portuguese, in the *German Quarterly* and in the *French Review*, the journals of the professional associations of the teachers of those languages.

In general the issues seem to center about the point in the curriculum at which literature should be introduced, the relevance of literary studies to the needs and interests of the language learner, the content of the literary curriculum (whether it is to be limited to belles lettres), the use of simplified or abridged editions, and the role of literature in the transmission of the target culture.

All of this suggests that a considerable amount of uncertainty surrounds the question of the role of literature in foreign-language instruction, not only in connection with English as a foreign language but with foreign-language instruction in general. Moreover, most of the discussion concerning this matter has been somewhat fragmented. Much of it has dealt with only a single question or issue: the vocabulary problem, the efficacy of abridgment or simplification, and so on. There has been little attempt to explore the question in depth from as many angles as possible. It will be the purpose in the chapters which follow to present a consideration of the question that will be as free from bias as possible and one which will give due regard to a number of relevant factors which are rarely dealt with. Although the primary focus will be on the English-teaching situation in the Asian countries, the very nature of the approach will insure some attention to other parts of the world as well.

Before setting out on this somewhat ambitious course, we must clarify certain fundamental assumptions about the teaching of language and literature, for the purpose of furnishing a general context for the inquiry. Too often, so it would seem, educational discussions are carried on and curricular decisions are made with insufficient awareness of the beliefs about education, about learning, and about the particular subject matter under discussion which underlie the discussion.

To draw upon illustrations outside of the field of language, it is quite clear that the history teacher, requiring a class to memorize a list of key dates, does so not out of an inherent sadism but rather to establish a few chronological benchmarks which will serve as a context for other events. Justification for either the old or the new mathematics rests upon different concepts of the learning process and varying assessments of what is mathematically important. And in the teaching of language it is clear that a concept of language as habit-governed oral response to external stimuli would lead to oral drill in the classroom, whereas a view of language as a creative process would call for a quite different type of classroom activity.

Unfortunately, teachers are often too pressed for time to consider such underlying premises about the subject matter and the learning process as they go about their daily tasks. Even when they discuss matters of curriculum and teaching technique, these are generally dealt with in terms of *what* is to be done in the classroom and *how* the teacher is to perform rather than what would seem to be a due regard for *why* the teacher is to do what he does when he does it. Questions of *what* and *how* are matters of teacher training. Questions which ask *why* are of a higher order. They fall into the province of teacher education, and can be dealt with only in the broader terms of clearly stated beliefs and underlying principles.

The necessity for a recognition and clarification of general principle is all the more evident here because of the tendency to deal on an ad hoc basis with the whole complex of questions which inevitably arise in any consideration of the place of literature in the foreign language curriculum. As we have already seen, discussions of the topic have been so fragmented as to preclude a consistent and overall approach to the problem.

It is the purpose here to set forth the assumptions which would seem to be important to any consideration of the place of literature in the English curriculum when it is taught as a foreign or second language. Certain of these may seem self-evident; others may come as something of a surprise. A brief statement of these principal premises will suffice here. A more detailed presentation will follow later in the study as each of them is taken up in turn.

A. The position of English within a country, that is, as a foreign language, or a second language, or a language of study has an important bearing upon the determination of the aims of English instruction in that country.
B. The aims of English instruction within a country will influence the place and treatment of English within the total curriculum, and this in turn will determine the role of literature in English instruction.
C. The way in which the native literature is taught in the country and its place in the general educational scheme establishes a set of expectations and restrictions which will inevitably have a powerful influence upon the teaching of a foreign literature.
D. The availability of English literature in translations, particularly in terms of the identity of the authors and works translated, serves as an index of public taste and interest which should be taken into consideration in planning the literary portion of the English curriculum.
E. The particular nature of the English vocabulary and the well-established facts of word frequency and distribution must be taken into consideration in the selection of literary works to be studied, in the classroom approach to these works, and in connection with whatever decisions are to be made about the use of simplified or abridged versions.
F. The role of literature in transmitting the target culture must be realistically appraised in terms of curricular aims and teaching procedures.

There are other matters which might have been listed here, but the six which have been included seem basic to the question and the spirit in which the inquiry will be conducted. At a time of heightened uncertainty about language-teaching philosophy, techniques, and approaches, it is of paramount importance that a spirit of cool rationality and unfettered inquiry be not only preserved but strengthened. Only in such an atmosphere can sound educational decisions ensue.

CHAPTER 2

The Role
of English
in the Nation
and in the Schools

THE ENGLISH LANGUAGE is notable not so much for the number of persons who speak it as a first or native language, but rather for its wide distribution throughout the world. With respect to sheer numbers it lags far behind Chinese and does not far surpass Russian and possibly Hindi. Yet no other language is firmly entrenched as a native language on four continents, with some additional use on a fifth. It is this factor which, perhaps more than any other, accounts for its importance not only as a native but as an auxiliary language as well.

As an auxiliary language the role of English may vary considerably. If the native language of a country is one of the seven or eight so-called languages of wider communication, the English language has little more than a circumscribed supplementary function to perform. This could be equally true if several languages are spoken natively within the country and one of these is a language of wider communication.

At the opposite extreme, one may conceive of a situation where several mutually unintelligible languages, none of them widely spoken, have been native to a country which in the past had been a colonial possession of an English-speaking nation. Under these circumstances, communication with the world outside, and even much of the communication within the country, beyond narrowly confined local or regional boundaries, will depend upon English. In fact, much of the functioning of the country will call for a widespread mastery of English on the part of a significant portion of the total population.

What have just been described are, of course, polar opposites, and actual situations in countries may be taken as points on a continuum which ranges from one extreme to the other. Probably in no two countries is the situation identical. Nevertheless it is possible to recognize three broad categories with respect to the national role of the English language, the part it plays in the affairs of a nation.

In the first of the two country portraits given at the outset of this chapter, English functions as what may be termed a foreign language. This would be true, for example, of the place of English in countries such as Japan, Germany, or Italy. Each of these countries is wholly capable of functioning without the English language. It can operate politically and economically in its national language. English is certainly helpful but by no means a *sine qua non* in the conduct of international diplomacy or international commercial activity. As far as the individual living within the country is concerned, a knowledge of English is an attractive cultural accomplishment; for some, it may even have certain practical advantages, but the proportion of persons in such a country who must have a command of English in order for that country to get along is very small indeed.

Nor does the situation differ materially in a country such as Peru, where Spanish—a language of wider communication—and Quechua are the two current languages. For those who have been born into a Quechua-speaking environment, it is merely necessary to learn the other language of the country in order to enhance their communication potential. Again, a knowledge of English brings with it certain advantages, essentially those which have already been suggested in the foregoing paragraph. Its position again is that of a foreign language, supplementary rather than basic to the social structure of the country.

The term which is applied to the role of English in the second of the country situations described at the outset of this chapter is that of a second language. The term *second* may be understood in two senses. Chronologically, it is the language which is acquired after the speaker has mastered his native language or mother tongue, or at least after he has made a good start toward doing so. Socially, it is a language which not only supplements whatever language may be native to the area or to the speaker but in a sense is virtually necessary to conduct the affairs of the country. For example, in Ghana the principal indigenous languages are Fanti and Twi. In addition, both Ewe and Ga are used by large numbers. Since all of these native tongues are spoken by only minorities of the population, the sole language the people have in common is English. Consequently, to the extent that internal communication within the country is a desideratum, vast numbers of speakers must be bilingual in English and their native language.

Bilingualism here implies that much of the business of government will be carried on in the one common language. Parliamentary deliberation will be conducted in English; unquestionably one version of the statutes will be written in English. In addition, English will serve as the language of the courts, of the publication of executive orders, and reports of government bureaus. It may well be the language in which many or all of the commercial transactions are carried on, including the writing of business correspondence and the drawing up of contracts, not to mention word-of-mouth business negotiations. English may be the language in which certain ceremonial functions are conducted, ranging from church services, baptisms, weddings, and funerals to the celebration of national holidays and the inauguration or induction into office of governmental functionaries.

Beyond this, English may be wholly or in part the language employed by the communications media of the country: newspapers, magazines, radio, television, motion pictures. It may be the language in which some of the literature of the country is written, of plays which are produced. Finally, it may be wholly or in part the language of instruction in the schools, a matter which will be dealt with more fully later on in this chapter. Let it be noted, however, that the role of English in a country situation such as the one which has just been described virtually commits a country to the recognition of bilingualism as a national policy. In a case like this, the so-called second language is in essence one half of a bilingual pairing.

Again, a number of variations of one kind or another on this pattern must be acknowledged. In the Philippines, for example, the situation is complicated by the recent emergence of Pilipino, a national language based largely upon Tagalog. In a sense English is a third language here, or at least in those parts of the country which are not natively Tagalog-speaking, for the people there will have acquired the local language first, be it Bisayan, Ilocano, or what not. Yet in terms of its position in the national society, English must fulfill all of the functions of a second language. This is also true in many parts of India, those in particular where Hindi is not the prevailing local language.

English may take on a third-language status when it acquires increased importance in a country in which another world language is already serving a second-language function. This has been the case, for example, in Vietnam, where French formerly filled the role of a second language with total adequacy, and still does for many of those who received their education prior to, or even shortly after, the withdrawal of the French from Indochina. With the increase in American influence during the past two decades, English has become a rival to French for second-language status, though probably not to the point of displacing it. The same situation applies, though possibly to a lesser degree, in Laos.

English has run into a somewhat similar set of circumstances in the countries of Francophone Africa, except that here the question of the displacement of French as a second language does not arise. However, each of the African countries in which French is used alongside the native language has some ties with, or finds it necessary to communicate with, other African countries in which English is the second language. In situations such as these, the use of the third language is considerably more limited than that of the second, especially in numbers of speakers. It is not assumed that more than a minority of the population will be trilingual.

At one time the role of English in any country where it was not spoken natively was conceived of as falling into one of the two categories which have just been described, English as a foreign language or English as a second language. More recently a third classification has been recognized as well, that of a "library language" or language of study, as I prefer to call it.

The argument for recognizing "library language" or language of study as a category runs somewhat as follows: There are countries where English does not fulfill all of the second-language functions but its importance goes beyond that of foreign-language status. One may take a country such as Thailand as a case in point. English is not an official language there, although it is important commercially. It is not the language of instruction in the elementary or secondary schools, although it is a universally required foreign language; the public school pupils begin to study it at the outset of the upper primary level, namely the fifth grade, for a total of eight years. Many private schools begin the study of English one or two years earlier. Thus there is considerable exposure to the language even though it is not used to teach other subjects.

At the same time, as is the case in many countries where it is a second language, English does serve the purpose of opening "a window to the world," as Nehru phrased it, at least for all those whose interests and concerns transcend the purely local or national. For those whose intellectual reach is of that magnitude, the Thai language is not likely to be the vehicle which will serve them adequately. For example, a new research work written in English in such fields as microbiology, geophysics, or survey-research techniques is likely to be translated into Japanese within months of its appearance. It is not likely to be translated into Thai at all, in large part because the size of the potential market would not justify the outlay of the translating and publishing costs. Moreover, there still seems to be considerable uncertainty among the

Thai as to whether their vocabulary can be successfully adapted, not only to certain of these emerging new disciplines but even to those which are older, uncompounded, and unhyphenated. In a sense, this situation affects the professional and scientific groups in the country, or one might even say the entire intellectual community.

But the problem is not limited to reading newly published materials. If this were the case, the term "library language" would be descriptively adequate. In order for the country to keep up with these fields, with this expanding knowledge, certain advanced students and established professionals will have to study abroad, a large share of them in English-speaking countries. For this group, a mastery of all four language skills, not merely that of reading, will be necessary. In addition, foreign scholars knowledgeable in the field may be brought to the host country. It is most likely that they will have to lecture in their native language—or even in English if it is not their native language—which will add oral comprehension as a necessary skill to the reading knowledge which has already been deemed necessary. Students may have to prepare papers and reports, in English naturally enough if the lecturer is to read and interpret them, which adds writing as a third necessary element. And certainly, students will have to respond to their instructor, again in his own language, thus creating a need for the fourth of the language skills, namely speaking.

In conclusion, we find ourselves at a point where the situation demands control of all four language skills. It will not be as extensive, perhaps, as is the case with English as a second language in that a smaller proportion of the population is affected and the range of subject matter is more restricted. Nevertheless, within these limits a high degree of competence is called for. In the light of all these considerations, "language of study" seems a far more appropriate term than "library language."

Like any other scheme of classification, the threefold one which has been suggested tends to oversimplify matters. Not everything is so neatly cut and dried as it has been presented here. In some countries where English has foreign-language status, Poland for example, it is one of three or four languages which may be studied and happens not to be the language with the greatest number of elections in the secondary schools. In Japan, on the other hand, languages other than English are offered only in the Upper Secondary schools and are probably not studied very extensively. Here it is possible that the popularity of English may be too great, and that in view of the country's geographical and political future, it should not so completely overshadow other foreign languages which ought also to be studied.

With respect to the other end of the scale, the position of English as a second language would seem to be firmer in the Philippines than it is in India. In other areas, such as Malaysia, English seems to be shifting from a second-language position to that of a language of study.

What is unquestionably needed for each of these countries is first of all a sociolinguistic survey which will define as accurately as possible the role which English plays within the country and how its role compares with that of other languages which may be encountered. For this the forthcoming survey of the place and uses of English in Jordan [Harrison 1977] would conveniently serve as a model. In addition, it would be most desirable to have for each country an exposition of the place of English within the public educational system as cogent, comprehensive, and perceptive as the study *Japan's Second Language* by Dr. John Brownell (1967).

Since it is a function of an educational system, particularly one which is publicly supported, to serve the needs and interests, present and future, of the nation, we move naturally from a consideration of the various roles English may play in the countries of the world to its place in their educational systems in the light of these roles.

Let us begin with those countries where English has the place of a second language. Almost by definition, this establishes bilingualism as an educational objective for a large share of the population, if not for all of it. This is the case, for example, in the Philippines, where the place of English is set forth in a *Constitution on Language*, and in accordance with this, a bilingual educational policy is defined and detailed in Order no. 25, S-1974 of the Department of Education and Culture. There are documents and orders of this nature in virtually every country where English is formally recognized either as an official or as an auxiliary language, and any final determination of the place of English within the educational system, or of the place of literature within the English curriculum, must take into consideration the documented position of the ministry, government, and constitution.

At all events, if anything like bilingualism is to be achieved, the schools must provide a means of saturating their pupils with experiences in English. This means that the teaching of English must begin early and continue throughout the entire period of schooling, or at least close to it—even into higher education. It means also that experience with the language must be intensified by using English as a medium of instruction, either wholly or in part. This is, in fact, the case in most countries where English has second-language status. English instruction begins early, usually in the primary grades, and does extend to many of the other subjects in the curriculum.

With English instruction spread over a dozen years or more and extending into subject-matter areas other than the language itself, there is clearly time and room in the curriculum for the study of literature, if such study were judged to be a means of realizing an educational objective of bilingualism. If a stated aim of bilingualism implies as well an acquaintance with two cultures, it could be argued that some experience with the literature of a country does constitute a bridge to its culture. Admittedly, the reading and class consideration of English or American literature is not in and of itself a passport to Anglo-Saxon culture. Nevertheless, literature can be made to fulfill a cultural objective if careful plans are made toward this end, involving the choice of literary selections and manner of presentation. Needless to say, a set of academic lectures on the topic will fail of their purpose; here we are in the realm of the affective and not the cognitive.

It must also be remembered that in many countries where English has a second-language status, there are creative writers who use English as a vehicle for some or all of their work: Narayan in India, Emmanuel Torres in the Philippines, Chinua Achebe in Nigeria are examples which readily come to mind. Certainly acquainting the student with the current literary output of his countrymen is not only a justifiable but a praiseworthy, if not an essential, educational aim. Unfortunately, as the English curriculum is now organized in many countries where English has the role of a second language, due consideration is not given to these native writers, for a variety of reasons. But certainly any realistic consideration of the general aims of education and of the second-language role of English within such a structure would seem to leave little doubt that some kind of experience with literature written in English could properly claim a place in the curriculum. The question of what that place should be will be taken up later.

Let us now examine the situation at the opposite end of the scale, English as a foreign language. The objectives of teaching English in a country where it is considered a foreign rather than a second language are much more modest and do not differ markedly from the purposes of foreign language instruction within the American educational system. In a report on the teaching of English in Japan, prepared for a regional meeting of experts on the teaching of English in Asia (1971), Mr. Takaharu Kumida explains that "most of the Japanese people wish they could hear, speak, read, and write English. Many of them are actually endeavoring to master English as a means of communication with English speaking peoples" (p. 91). Notice that this is expressed in terms of a desire, however strong and general it may be, but not in terms of a necessity or a mandate. Moreover, in the official regulations as set forth in the Ministry of Education courses of study for both lower and upper secondary schools, one objective is: "Through English to help the pupils develop the understanding of the life and views of foreign people." Again, important as this aim is from a humanistic point of view, it is not an immediate bread-and-butter objective.

As a consequence, in what we may term EFL countries, the study of English begins later than it does where English has the role of a second language, usually in the secondary schools—lower secondary if a bipartite division is recognized. English is studied as a separate subject; it is not the language of instruction. In theory it may be one of a number of elective foreign languages, although in actual fact it usually outstrips its rivals in popularity. In general the exposure of the pupils to the language is much more limited than in an ESL country, both in and out of school. In some EFL countries, though it is not always true, the technical and vocational needs are somewhat less urgent than they are in ESL countries. Instructions for assembling or servicing electronic equipment clearly do not need to be written in English in countries such as Germany or Japan; it is more important that they be so written in Thailand or Sri Lanka.

Because the technical needs are often somewhat circumscribed, this would seem to leave more time for the realization of the cultural component in the modern-language curriculum, however that may be defined, especially for those students whose purpose in attending the secondary schools and the university is to acquire a liberal education rather than a somewhat narrowly oriented vocational or preprofessional training. In the extended study of a language such as English, exposure to the literature which has been produced in that language can make a valuable contribution to the realization of the cultural aim.

This leaves for our consideration the in-between countries, those in which English has the function of a language of study. Because of the clearly defined special needs of the students and their commitment to a rigorous preprofessional or professional program, it might seem on the surface as if literature as a part of the English curriculum could not be justified as readily as in either of the other two situations, and that whatever is selected for reading in such a situation should have a direct bearing upon the professional goals of the student.

Yet, if one takes a sufficiently broad view of literature, this does not necessarily follow. Much technical and scientific writing in English is notorious for its clumsiness and stylistic infelicity. Accordingly, there should be no objection to providing the student with examples of lucid and graceful prose which is expository in purpose, and which does draw its subject matter from the physical and social sciences. There is a considerable amount of this prose which is written for the cultivated reader who is not a professional in the particular field. A list would include much of the work of writers like William Beebe, John Lear, Norman Cousins, Buckminster Fuller, Ashley Montague—in short, the kind of writing one might expect to find in *Saturday Review* or *Scientific American*. Though not belletristic, this is literature in the broader sense.

Upon examination, then, it appears that there is a justifiable and a profitable place for literature in the English curriculum, irrespective of the role of the English language within the country, although it will differ in nature as the role of the language differs. It is equally clear that the place and the purpose of a literary component within the English curriculum will differ with the place and the purpose of teaching English. It is for this reason that official statements relative to the educational goals of the country, particularly with respect to the use of language, are important, and also whatever country curriculum may have been devised for the purpose of achieving these goals. They furnish a point of departure for the kind of thinking about foreign-language curricula and the place of literature in them that is necessary for a proper resolution of the issues that have been raised.

It is also important to note that the way in which literature in the foreign-language course is currently taught may not necessarily be the best way to proceed if one considers the function of English in the country curriculum in the way which has been suggested here. Once this function is clearly defined, it is then appropriate to review the content of the literature that is included in the program, the contribution it is intended to make to the development of the student, and the possible ways of presenting it so that it will realize its purpose. In considering the matter from this point of view, a number of questions arise, which we shall have to consider in some kind of order. The first of these, perhaps, should deal with the way in which the native literature is taught, since this will provide a background against which the teaching of a foreign literature may be considered.

CHAPTER 3
Teaching the
Native Literature

IT HAS ALREADY been stated as a premise that the teaching of the native literature within a country establishes something of a norm for the teaching of any literature. A brief explanation will be sufficient to demonstrate the pertinence of this observation.

In most countries, certainly, some consideration of the literature that is written in the native language (or languages) finds its way into the curriculum, some of it very early in the form of stories told to children or simple prose designed to develop the pupil's ability to read. Later on, there may be further exposure to the literature, both in the secondary schools and the university—for a variety of purposes. Much of this, possibly all but a part of the college and university courses, will form a part of the general educational experience of the student, including those who go on to become foreign-language teachers. Certainly, the memory of how the native literature was presented to them in the classroom will remain as a memory of their educational experience, and will tend to shape their own teaching of a foreign literature when they have the occasion and the opportunity to do so. Moreover, it is quite likely that the educational aims of teaching literature in the native language will influence the purposes for which literature is introduced into the foreign-language curriculum.

Since the experience of most teachers, either as students or as members of the profession, seldom ranges beyond a single country, it is not at all surprising that they assume the aims, procedures, and curriculum design in the teaching of literature in their own country to be the same as those which prevail elsewhere. They have little or no idea of the wide variation that is possible here. Yet, if the premise upon which we are proceeding is to be exploited to its fullest potential, it will be necessary to develop a mode of analyzing the various ways in which the native literature can be and is being taught.

Possibly the best place to begin is with literature as it is taught in the United States. The reason for doing so is that the range of variation in techniques and approaches is very broad, possibly broader than in any other country in the world, due partly to the lack of a centralized or federalized educational system, and partly because the atmosphere for educational experimentation has generally been favorable. We shall begin with the study of literature as it is carried on in higher education, try to arrive at some general conclusions about it, and go on to observe what modifications and additions will have to be made in these in order to accommodate them to the secondary and elementary school scene. Although our concern here is with the United States, American and British literature will be considered as constituting a single whole. The peculiar problems posed by the existence of at least two national literatures in English will be discussed briefly later on.

We must recognize first of all that departments of English concerned with the native literature are a development of the past one hundred years. A very few go back as much as a century and a quarter. Most of those in the English universities are even more recent. At the same time, the scholarly and critical study of English literature is at least four centuries old.

Prior to this, it was only the literature written in the classical languages which was considered worthy of formalized study. At that time, "classical" meant the literature of Greece and Rome: a somewhat culture-bound concept, to be sure, but one which led to certain educational practices which might today be considered reasonably modern. For example, the classical curriculum in both secondary school and college was in essence that which in modern terms might be called an area program in the ancient world. Euclid served as the textbook in mathematics. Herodotus, Thucydides, Caesar, and Tacitus were the source materials for the history of the area. The geography was that of the territory surrounding the Mediterranean. Science and philosophy found their way into the program as well, also in the form of ancient works. This, incidentally, illustrates one type of organizing principle which might be followed in the presentation of a foreign language and culture, one in which literature has a place in an integrated whole.

The classical curriculum which has been described was studied by only a small segment of the country's youth. At the turn of the century, the total secondary school enrollments amounted to no more than ten percent of the youth population in that age group; those in higher education approximately four percent. Possibly one-half of them elected the classical curriculum. They were not taught the native literature because it was assumed that a cultivated person would read it anyway.

The study of the native literature got its start with the development of a general or scientific curriculum, first in the secondary schools and later in the colleges and universities. As William R. Parker once somewhat playfully pointed out (1967), college English departments were the offspring of a broken marriage, that of philology and rhetoric. Rhetoric had an affair with Elocution; Philology changed its identity to Linguistics and took up an abode with Anthropology.

The figure is no longer quite so applicable as it was a decade ago, but it is true that philology once had a strong influence on the study of literature, with two notable results. The first was a strong emphasis on early literature, again on the assumption that anything written in the current idiom would be read anyway. The second was that literature was approached primarily from the point of view of its historical development. For many years the most popular college anthology of literary selections was one which bore the title *From Beowulf to Thomas Hardy*. The type of course which it served was called a survey.

The survey course was a fixture in the high schools as well as in the colleges. The secondary school survey was often spread over two years. Much the same ground was covered, possibly somewhat more intensively, in a single year in a college class. The list of authors often included many of decidedly minor rank. Selections were generally brief. The focus of the interpretive and explanatory materials was upon external details, information *about* the writer and his works. Such teaching aids, like the scholarship of the time, were concerned primarily with historical matters: the influence of Boethius upon Chaucer, Shakespeare's use of the commedia del arte, French and Jacobean elements in Restoration comedy. This was the philological method, modeled after the pattern of German scholarship.

At first glance this would seem to be a somewhat remote and arid approach to selections which in their time had been intended by their authors to move the readers profoundly. It did have the virtue of promoting an evolutionary concept of literary development, which was generally useful at the time. On the other hand, it did present certain difficulties. By maintaining a chronological sequence of selections, it forced the student to begin with the oldest and therefore the most difficult specimens of the language to read and to understand. Moreover, the selections were treated as specimens of literary, and sometimes even of linguistic, history rather than in and for themselves.

In the 1920s the grip of the totally historical approach began to loosen. There developed in its place a scheme of organization and presentation based upon literary types and forms, or genres. In the colleges this tended to lead to separate courses in the novel, the drama, the short story, the essay, and so on. In the secondary schools the prevailing tendency was to plan a progression presumably suited to the developing tastes and maturity of the student. Very often such a sequence began with selections in which the interest was almost wholly narrative. A variety of types and forms might be included—narrative poems, short story, the novel of romance or adventure. A second stage introduced the student to the presentation of character as a focal point, again emphasizing prose narrative but including drama as well. This was followed by an exploration of reflective and personal literature: the essay, some autobiographical writing, the lyric. The chronological survey was reserved for the fourth or final year, and of course became even more sketchy than it had been before.

From time to time modifications of the survey developed, in an effort to make it more palatable and more relevant. Two of these were especially influential upon later developments in the teaching of English literature. The first was the substitution of longer selections from fewer and more important authors for the variegated snippets which had come to constitute the normal survey fare. The second was the development of the backward historical approach, beginning with contemporary or near-contemporary writers and proceeding by consecutive stages to a consideration of the earlier works. This, of course, had the pedagogical advantage of beginning with the relatively familiar and of introducing the student gradually to the linguistic and cultural difficulties imposed by the passage of time. On the college level, the impact of the so-called New Criticism diverted attention from historical and linguistic considerations to the literary selection as a work of art. Crocean aesthetics emphasized the literary experience. Almost everything here combined to overcome and set aside what was perceived to be the weakness of the historical approach as it had been practiced.

Moreover, as the century went into its fourth and fifth decades, American secondary and even higher education embraced ever-increasing numbers, exceeding by far the small elite group who were in the schools at the outset of the century. The educational process shifted from one of raising the student body up to the level of their parents and environment to one of developing them to a point beyond that represented by their elders and their surroundings. Along with this change came the realization that nothing in the previous experience of many of these students would have taught them how to do the specialized reading that is required in order to assure some kind of response to literature. This gave rise to the type of introductory literature courses that tried to teach the student how to read a poem, to get at its meaning or significance and to respond to it, to read a novel and be able to identify and understand its theme, to read a play and to see the stage and its trappings in the mind's eye.

As school enrollments grew to include an even larger proportion of the youth population, many educators began to question whether the best of our literature could mean much of anything to the children of the economically disadvantaged. This resulted in an increasing emphasis on the contemporary and on what was believed to be relevant—themes, settings, characters with whom the pupils could identify: *West Side Story* rather than *Romeo and Juliet*. It was equally evident that the previously held assumption to the effect that modern literature would be read anyway was no longer valid.

At the same time representatives of the ethnic minorities in the schools and colleges began to demand a voice in the educational process and in particular in the selection of materials to be read. The immediate effect of this was the inclusion of material by black authors, and at higher levels of education the development of courses in Black Literature and in Black Studies as well. Further extension to Chicano, American Indian, and other ethnic groups seems imminent. In a sense this constitutes a fragmentation of what was once considered to be a fairly unified body of material (except for the special problem of American literature, which will be considered later in this chapter). The fragmentation has been aggravated by the development of countless mini-courses which deal with small specific bits of content or particular problems. For example, the 1972 issue of the State of Hawaii's *Language Arts Course Guide* lists some thirty-two elective course offerings at the secondary level, including such topics as Comparative Folklore, the Language of War, Literature from the Bible, Polynesian Literature, Science Fiction, and Literature of the Future. What has really disappeared in all this is the evolutionary or positivistic concept of literary history.

It is only natural that different observers viewing the same phenomenon or development over a period of time should see it as having different antecedents and as representing different tendencies. For a long time we have lacked an authoritative history of the teaching of English in the United States. This need has now been fulfilled by Arthur N. Applebee's *Tradition and Reform in the Teaching of English: A History* (1974). In his historical sketch of the subject, Applebee points to certain traditions originally influential in the United States that deserve mention here because they apparently are still powerful educational forces elsewhere. One of these is a strong ethical tradition which determined the content of such early educational standbys as the *New England Primer*, Noah Webster's blue-backed spelling textbooks, and the McGuffey readers. As Applebee summarizes the situation (p. 5):

> The *Primer* spread a common catechism, Webster's *Institute* advanced a common system of spelling and promoted a chauvinistic nationalism, McGuffey's readers created a literary heritage, even if one based on fragments and precis. This sense of an ethical and cultural heritage has certainly remained as one of the major goals of the teaching of literature, though later generations of teachers would come to question the kind of heritage a collection of excerpts could offer.

In addition, Applebee also sees the growth of English studies at an advanced level as owing its first impetus to a group of devoted educators "who divorced the studies of rhetoric and oratory from their early roots in grammar during roughly the same period that grammar was itself becoming an important school subject. . . . Throughout the nineteenth century, 'rhetoric,' 'analysis,' and 'criticism' usually indicated much the same course of study, in which a literary text would be critically examined to insure that it conformed with the prescriptive rules of grammar and rhetoric, all in the ultimate service of the student's own speaking and writing skills" (pp. 8, 9).

Applebee traces the rise of literary history as it emerged in the mid-nineteenth century, and also sees as important the development of a non-academic interest in literature, fostered largely through literary and debating societies and the lecture platform. This leads him to conclude (p. 14) that "by 1865, English studies had become a part of all three major traditions. Though in each case the study of English was subordinate to other goals, there was for the first time the possibility that all of these traditions might be united within the teaching of a single subject. And this is what happened in the following decades: English studies increasingly found ways to claim the intellectual strength of the classical tradition, the moral strength of the ethical tradition, and the utilitarian strength of the nonacademic tradition."

This summary is important for our purposes because, as we shall see, many of these elements are still present in the teaching of the native literature in other countries. It would not be to the point here to trace all the vicissitudes of the teaching of English literature in the United States over the past century, the movements and countermovements, the shifts in aim and in theory. It might be worthwhile, however, to indicate where we are at present. Possibly the following statement sums up as well as anything can the position taken by those who may be considered abreast of current developments in the teaching of the native literature.

"Today many teachers invite students to say how they as individuals respond to a work of literature: what it says to them and about their lives, about other human beings, and human life in general." This would seem to combine the concept of literature as experience with the present demand for relevance, for immediate significance in what is read.

Again in the interest of a clear understanding of the aim of the foregoing section of this chapter, let me repeat that the purpose of this analysis of the teaching of the native literature in the United States has been to illustrate the vast range and variety of philosophies and procedures that have come to be associated with the subject, and that against this American background, much of what goes on elsewhere can be identified.

It is equally important to recognize that the way in which the native literature is dealt with in the educational system depends to a marked extent upon the nature of that literature. In those countries where there is a vast amount of literature, the product of a long classical tradition going back several centuries, something like the philological approach is likely to prevail. As one of my informants explained the situation, "A Chinese teacher plays the triple roles of an annotator, philosopher, and historian. He is on the order of a Confucian scholar." The same observation would apply with equal force to Japan and India. In a quite different guise, perhaps, the philological tradition will also be found in a fair number of European countries, as a residue of the German scholarly approach.

At the other extreme one must consider those countries which have only just recently adopted a writing system and the bulk of whose literature is oral, and orally transmitted from generation to generation. This would be true, for example, in areas like the Trust Territories and the Cook Islands. The present concern in them is that the recently adopted models of Western education should not operate in a way which will eliminate all vestiges of the native culture. In order to avoid this, native story material is included in the curriculum almost from the very beginning of the child's school career. Legends take the form of drama in which historical events are enacted, and songs and chants usually accompany them. Problems often arise here in connection with the supply of authentic literary material, its extent and its adherence to tradition. Very often, as in the Cook Islands at present, the educational authorities find that they must rely upon a council of elders with extensive knowledge of the folk literature and history. Here, in essence, the teaching of the native literature serves a cultural purpose.

Another type of situation is represented by those countries which, for one reason or another, have only recently developed a native literature in what is now the country language. In the case of Indonesia, the elementary school pupil is introduced to animal fables, which have a long history in that part of the world. But, as is often the case, the fables are introduced with two ulterior motives: to teach reading and to teach listening comprehension. The selections which are read by junior high school students are confined to whatever has been written since Bahasa Indonesia became the official language. It is only in the senior high school that the student is introduced to the wealth of material which exists in Sumatran, Javanese, and other languages of the archipelago. My Indonesian informants conclude that on the whole literature does not have a very significant place in the school experience of the student. Another country where the native literature is of relatively recent origin is Malaysia, and here again one can scarcely say that a native tradition for the teaching of Malaysian literature has developed.

The case of Korea, though different in certain details, does present some striking similarities as well. There appear to be some fine classical literary works, but they are couched in language that is quite beyond the grasp of the secondary school pupil. The classical works are taught at college level, in a manner not markedly different from that which has already been noted for such countries as China, Japan, and India. Aside from this early material, there had not been many literary works meriting serious study until the early twentieth century, when there appears to have been something of a literary renaissance. As an indication of what actually goes on in a university literature class, the following account by a product of the university system is helpful:

> The professor had prepared the student for the advance lesson by previewing the vocabulary, structure, and the theme or ideas. At the beginning of the class hour, the professor gives some background about the writer and the work itself. The several students are asked to read and paraphrase some passages of the text, often with the help of other students, or else the professor does this himself. Students are asked to summarize the entire selection. Then there will be a discussion on the ideas and themes of the work, and the students are expected to ask questions. Finally the professor assigns the homework, which may be a composition on a topic related to the lesson or further reading and summary of the work in question.

It will be noticeable to those familiar with the American scene that the procedure here does not differ materially from the run-of-the-mine approach to literature in the United States, either in an English class or one in a foreign language. It is not representative of the best that we can do. Yet there is some student participation here, although on a somewhat unimaginative and mechanical basis.

Since this can scarcely pretend to be a survey of all the various approaches to teaching a native literature, we may as well conclude our brief résumé at this point. The intent here has merely been to suggest that there are many different ways of teaching the native literature, and that these different ways are logical outcomes of the expressed purposes of education, the kind of literature that the country in question possesses, and the role of the literature in the life and experience of the people. These vary tremendously.

At the present time what facts are known about the teaching of the native literature are so fragmentary that no easy generalizations about country or world areas are possible. It is more than likely that any educator who interests himself in this problem and its implications for the teaching of foreign literatures or even for education in general will have to conduct his own factual investigation. The purpose of the foregoing pages has been to suggest some avenues of pursuit and some possible implications of the findings which may turn up.

It must be emphasized again that the way in which the native literature is being taught in any country inevitably imposes a pattern and a set of limitations in the way that literature will be taught in a foreign-language course. Not in an absolutely strict and rigid sense, of course, but in concept and approach generally. The extent to which this may occur is well illustrated by the reaction of a Japanese teacher of English to whom it was suggested that he emulate the practices of some of his native American colleagues in eliciting responses from his students. He commented, "It is perfectly all right for Mr. Smith to wave his arms as if he were directing an orchestra in teaching sentence patterns, but as a native Japanese, I can't do that. And besides, I am much more interested in the ideas of life and death as they are expressed in English literature than I am in the position of *often*, *seldom*, and *never* in a sentence."

I have already suggested that the special relationship which American literature bears to that produced in England poses a problem which exists irrespective of whether English is being taught as a foreign or a native language. The issue can be simply stated: Shall the literature of the United States and the literature of Britain be considered as separate entities or as parts of a single whole? In a larger sense, of course, the problem is not confined to the literature of the United States; it extends not only to that written in Canada, Australia, New Zealand, South Africa, and the West Indies, where English is a first language, but also to India, the Philippines, Ghana, Uganda, and Sierra Leone, where English has second-language status. It poses the question as to whether we should be thinking of English literature or of literature written in English.

Of all the national literary activity mentioned in the preceding paragraph, the literature written in the United States is the oldest and most extensive. In the interest of economy, therefore, the ensuing discussion of the problem shall be confined to that, although the same issues arise in connection with any of the countries which have been named, or even Scotland and Ireland, for that matter.

Although American literature is the oldest of the English literatures produced outside of the former area of the United Kingdom, it covers a very brief span of time compared with that of England. English literature, in the restricted belletristic sense, covers a period of some twelve centuries, from the eighth to the present. In contrast, but for an occasional scattered exception, the American colonies produced scarcely any belles lettres until the end of the eighteenth century. From Charles Brockden Brown and Philip Freneau to the present is no more than two hundred years. Such gigantic English literary figures as Chaucer, Shakespeare, Dryden, Pope, and Dr. Johnson all flourished before there was any American product which might properly be called literature, and so did the four great eighteenth-century novelists, Richardson, Fielding, Smollett, and Sterne. From one point of view, therefore, we are talking about quite unequal entities.

For the past century and a half, however, the American literary output has been impressive, both for its quantity and its quality. Essayists such as Emerson and Thoreau were bold and venturesome in their thought. Whitman and Poe, for entirely different reasons, were powerful poetic figures, and Poe was a master craftsman of the short story as well. Hawthorne, Melville, Samuel Clemens—each lent his peculiar genius to the novel. They have had worthy successors in the present century with such figures as Fitzgerald, Hemingway, and Faulkner. American drama began somewhat slowly (but then, England was scarcely notable for its eminence in this field in the nineteenth century), yet since that time Eugene O'Neill, Tennessee Williams, Thornton Wilder, and Arthur Miller have made outstanding contributions to the American stage.

The principal question that arises in connection with this whole problem is whether the American literary eminences who have been mentioned in the preceding paragraph fit neatly into what one might think of as a mainstream of literature written in English, or whether there is so much in them that is peculiarly and characteristically American that they ought to be studied by themselves. Generally in American colleges and universities, where the aim may be more than merely learning to read literature with insight, and extending to an appreciation of the historical and cultural context in which it is produced, American literature is studied either separately or as part of an American Civilization and Culture program. It used to be taken up separately in the secondary schools as well, though this may be less true now. We seem not to have been able to stretch our thinking sufficiently to see American and

English literature as constituting a single broad panorama. It is interesting to note that the same observation may be made with reference to Spanish literature of the Iberian peninsula and Spanish literature of the Americas. They are, almost without exception, taught separately in the United States.

Unquestionably, from this hasty survey of practices in teaching the native literature, a number of ways in which the teaching of literature in the context of a foreign-language course might be changed and improved have already suggested themselves. We shall hold these in abeyance for the present while we undertake a similar review of the teaching of foreign literatures.

CHAPTER 4

The Teaching
of Literature
in Foreign-Language
Classes

JUST AS WE BEGAN our survey of the teaching of native literatures with an account of American practices, we shall follow the same pattern in undertaking a review of the teaching of foreign literatures, and for the same reasons. Classroom practices in the United States provide a very broad range of variation against which the situation in other countries may be profitably viewed.

We have already seen that the teaching of the modern languages in the United States developed as an outgrowth of the teaching of the classical languages. The same may be said for the teaching of literature in connection with both. At the outset, literary selections were used, at least in the secondary schools, to give practice and to develop the pupil's facility in reading. There was, in fact, an almost universal sequence in Latin: Caesar's *Gallic Wars*, Cicero's *Orations*, and Virgil's *Aeneid* in the second, third, and fourth years of instruction respectively. This was justifiable in terms of increasing difficulty, a progression from straightforward narration to rhetorically ornate and argumentative discourse to poetry. The *Anabasis* was a corresponding staple of the course in ancient Greek.

In the colleges and universities, courses tended to concentrate on the study of single authors: Ovid, Livy, Catullus, Seneca, Plautus in Latin; for Greek, Sophocles, Aeschylus, Aristophanes, Plato, Aristotle, Homer, Herodotus. Survey courses in the classics were and are still something of a rarity. This may be explained in part because the curricular pattern in the classics was fixed before the German concept of developmental literary history got its grip on American scholarship. Another factor which had some bearing on the curriculum was that the purpose of classical studies was to put the student into direct contact with the best that had been thought and said—to borrow the Arnoldian terminology—in the course of the development of Western civilization. Considered in these terms, chronological sequence was a matter of little importance, and the notion of historical development was of no more than minor interest.

The study of the modern languages in the United States, though employing similar classroom practices, arose from motives somewhat different from those of the classical languages, and in fact the motives were not the same for all parts of the colonies. In New England, for example, French was considered important because Calvin and other Protestant theologians had written in that language. In the South, somewhat later to be sure, Thomas Jefferson's enthusiasm for French rationalism and French political ideas weighed heavily as a motivating factor. German, developing still later, tended to be studied partly out of ethnic interest and partly because of the enthusiasm for German educational models and German scientific research in the early and mid-nineteenth century. In either event, the overriding aims were not at all literary at the beginning.

In these early stages of modern-language instruction, whenever literature was read in the classroom, it was designed to serve as a pathway to facility in reading and in mastering the language generally, as had been the case with Latin. As early as John Locke's *Some Thoughts Concerning Education* (1693), fables were thought to be appealing literary fare for children, especially if the circumstances did not permit "talking the language into them," that is to say providing total immersion with native speakers. And, of course, with the works of La Fontaine, there was a body of French material ready for use. This practice became popular in the United States, where the first use of fables as content material in French goes back to 1784. In 1829 Antoine Bolmar published *A Selection of One Hundred of Perrin's Fables Accompanied with a Key*. The so-called key was an interlinear translation, of which more will be said later.

At the same time, many people were firm in their belief that the French spoken at the Comédie Française was superior to anything else for its purity and elegance. As a result they concluded that there was no better way to learn French than to attend the performances. In 1778 John Adams reported that he went often to the theater, taking with him a printed copy of the play and comparing it line for line and word for word with what was spoken on the stage. But, if one were not in a position to attend the theater, one could always read the play. In this way the comedies of Molière became part of the literary fare of the French course. And once comedy was there, it was easy enough to go to the tragedies of Racine and Corneille as well.

Possibly the strangest choice for a literary text was *Télémaque* by Fénelon, a French religious mystic of the eighteenth century, a narrative purporting to recount the adventures of Telemachus in searching for his father, but given all manner of allegorical interpretation. For classroom purposes this was usually published as an interlinear text and was very popular throughout most of the nineteenth century. Its use came about in this way: it had been published in the United States as early as 1784, but the first to gloss it for teaching purposes was one Jean Jacques Jacotot, in 1822. As Professor of French at the University of Louvain, he had perfected a system to teach French to his Flemish- and Dutch-speaking students which he called "émancipation intellectuelle." Using an edition of *Télémaque,* with a translation into Dutch on the opposite or facing pages, he required his students to memorize all of the first book, to repeat it from memory every day, and then go on to the following books. Then the students were to speak like the characters in the book, but in slightly different contextual situations. From these activities the students were expected to derive all of the pertinent grammatical knowledge for themselves.

In a sense all of the procedures which have been described here illustrate the use of one literary text or another as a language-learning tool, a practice which has become a moot issue today.

During the period from 1875 to 1910, American educators developed a mechanism for measuring the equivalency of secondary school work to that done in college, namely what came to be called the Carnegie Unit. On the basis of this, one year of college work in a foreign language was counted as equal to two years in the secondary school. As a consequence, no student of a foreign language, even if he had had four years of it in high school, could enter a college course at a point more advanced than the beginning of third-year college work.

This resulted in a fairly sharp break between what was offered in the third and fourth years of the high school course (or the second year in college) and the beginning of the third year of college work, in all of the foreign languages that were offered. In the third and fourth high school years or the second college year, literary selections were taken up in a somewhat disconnected fashion. They appear to have been chosen—and in fact, the practice still continues—on the grounds of relative ease of reading, brevity, and presumed interest in and for themselves. The short stories of de Maupassant have been great favorites in French classes. In German courses the novella (something of a cross between the short story and the novel) seemed to be standard fare; Theodor Storm's *Immensee* was a great favorite.

From that point on, it was a matter of specialization. There were period courses: the *Sturm und Drang* in German, the *Siglo del Oro* in Spanish. There were genre courses (drama, short story); there were courses in individual authors (Goethe, Cervantes) or works (the *Chanson de Roland*). There were survey courses, covering the entire span of the literature, not unlike those which had developed in English literature. Departments of French developed a special type of approach, the *cours de civilisation*. Indeed, in every instance it was hoped that the pupil would absorb a feeling for the culture that was associated with the target language. For a number of reasons, this was rarely achieved.

For one thing, it is necessary to reckon with two concepts of culture, the belletristic and the anthropological. The former, that is to say culture in the Arnoldian sense, is often a matter of universals and is not tied to any one nation or language. The anthropological concept entails an examination into many aspects of the lives and values of the speakers of the target language, concerning which language teachers who were native Americans have tended and still tend to be naive. Conversely, native speakers of the target language, to the extent to which they were to be found in American schools and colleges, were correspondingly innocent about many aspects of Anglo-Saxon culture, and consequently unaware of the conflicts between the native and the target culture.

A survey of recent developments in the teaching of foreign literatures seems to reveal two. The first is a growth of courses in which the foreign literature is taught wholly or in part in translation. This has the obvious advantage of enabling the student to cover more ground in the same amount of time and to enhance his enjoyment by providing for him a direct contact with the literature instead of an exposure through the filter of an imperfectly mastered foreign language. It runs the risk of inadequacy of translation—to what extent can even the best of translations succeed in conveying the flavor of the original? It is only the very rare translation which succeeds in this—the Schlegel-Tieck translation of Shakespeare, according to some—but on the other hand the possible loss must be weighed against the advantages of increased coverage with less pain.

The second new development in this field is competently surveyed in an article by O. E. Dathorne entitled "Literary Studies in a Broader Context" (1974). The content of the article is, as he explains, "a response to a felt need of many of our high school and college students who do not feel an affinity to the traditional literary content of our courses" (p. 189). The so-called lack of affinity is accounted for as follows:

> Even the most cursory examination of the teaching of foreign literatures in the United States reveals that there is an emphasis on associating them with a European "metropolis." This tendency can easily be understood when one is dealing with Polish or German, Hindi or Chinese, or any language that is limited to one country or region. But regarding Portuguese, Spanish, and French in this way is a distortion, for these languages have an immediacy, albeit geographical, with the continental United States. In addition, one must remember that aspects of the new world process of acculturation, which has gone into these languages in this part of the world, give them definite significance for Americans. That even teachers of English Literature refuse to take either the writing of United States Blacks or Caribbean writers into consideration is particularly ludicrous. This makes for a sorry and paradoxical "parochialism." (p. 190)

After suggesting various Caribbean and African writers in each of the four languages for inclusion in the literary curriculum, Dathorne concludes:

> This article does not claim to be exhaustive. I have merely attempted to show that there is a rich reservoir of literature in Portuguese, English, Spanish, and French that relates very directly to us in the United States and is not being taught for a variety of reasons. Some of the problems that these writers relate parallel the issues that are pertinent in this country at present. The liberties that many of the authors take with the language of expression are not unlike the freedom American authors display. Fortunately they and we are removed from the stultifying environment of the "mother country" . . . .
> Seemingly then in this country we have vast potentialities for cultural maturity and the manifestation of a world destiny—the meeting point of all men at a common cultural rendezvous. This indicates that once and for all we can banish the narrow parochialism that has been part of the process of learning in other parts of the world. By extending the frontiers of literature, we enlarge imaginative possibilities; we leave our old world forbears alone and in search for a new thread of discovery, discard their static mold and regain a new focus of intensity, a novel turbulency of spirit. (pp. 215–216)

As in connection with the teaching of the native literature, I have again dealt with the American scene in considerable detail in order to illustrate the range of uses that the teaching of literature may serve and the various attitudes that may develop toward these uses. And again the American scene is a convenient starting point because of the variety to be encountered there, ranging from the traditionalism of the past century to the impatience with present methods which is so evident in the Dathorne article. With this range and variety in mind, let us now turn to what is known about the teaching of literature in connection with the English curriculum elsewhere.

Once more the distinction between English as a second language and English as a foreign language will serve as a point of departure. Because the foreign-language situation is essentially the simpler one, we shall begin there. A recent account of the teaching of English in the People's Republic of China (Ferguson 1975) may be taken as representing a concept of foreign-language study and a curriculum where literature would have the smallest possible part.

> In the United States, foreign languages are studied in part to give access to a different culture and way of life. Teaching materials, therefore, are expected to be as genuinely foreign as possible, based on actual language use in the countries where the language is spoken. In China, on the other hand, foreign languages are studied as weapons in the revolutionary struggle and the teaching materials for at least the first three years are based on life and thought in China, not in the foreign country. The student of English learns to talk about the Chinese countryside, to sing songs in honor of Chairman Mao and the Party . . . The Chinese student of English learns how to talk to foreign visitors about his own country; only the advanced student is exposed to texts from foreign countries—and then with political interpretation and commentary.

The selection of study materials with an ulterior political motive is generally characteristic of most Communist countries, and this extends to the choice of literature as well. Howard Fast's *Freedom Road* has probably enjoyed a greater popularity as material for literary study behind the iron curtain than it ever had in the United States, and this unquestionably applies to much of the work of Upton Sinclair as well. One book on the teaching of English, written for training colleges in Rumania, is careful to interpret most of Shakespeare in terms either of the class struggle or, as in the case of *Romeo and Juliet*, of the revolt of the younger generation against the tyranny of the older. *Huckleberry Finn* serves as documentation of the oppression of the blacks, with no suggestion of the internal conflict which goes on within Huck. A short story, "The Prize," appears in the textbooks of several Eastern European countries. The scene is laid in a New York metropolitan high school. A black girl has just won an essay contest, but because of her color the judges feel constrained not to award the prize to her. Just this much of the story is carefully included in all of the versions; what is universally omitted is the very moving conclusion, which portrays both the girl and her principal united in the tacit awareness that the time for this kind of discrimination has just about run its course and that hope for a new day is dawning.

It is only fair to recognize that if literary materials and approaches can serve as an instrument of political and social antagonism, they might just as easily be subverted in the opposite direction, as instruments of political advocacy, in short for propaganda, as the term is understood in English. One is more likely to encounter this in pamphlets and study guides prepared for distribution by governmental cultural and informational services rather than in host-country educational systems. For the most part, the tone of such material is so fatuous that scarcely anyone is misled or injured by it. Possibly one of the best records for open-mindedness in this connection is that of several of the West German state educational systems. East German literature is included in their syllabi without evidence of prejudicial selection or comment.

An interesting commentary on the situation in China prior to the Revolution comes from a student who received her education in Shanghai, studying there in British- and American-operated private schools (1974, private communication).

In both high school English and college level literature classes, the "Beowulf to Thomas Hardy" survey was offered. Literature was generally surveyed chronologically, but often with the earliest works studied last because of the difficulty of the language involved. I have very little impression of studying *Beowulf* in high-school English (although I know that I did); what stands out in my mind are parts of Chaucer's Canterbury Tales and some of Shakespeare's plays.

The college program in English literature offered a fair range of courses in American and English literary works. From a historical standpoint, British literature was covered more thoroughly. Little emphasis was placed on the current literary offerings of the day. The American Literature course did extend from Colonial literature to the writers of the 1920's and 1930's. Hemingway, O'Neill, Faulkner, and Steinbeck were studied as well as the poetry of Sandburg and Benet.

The manner in which these courses were taught in China differed greatly from the way in which an American college would have them presented. The lecture method was used throughout, even in courses in literary criticism. Feedback from students was in the form of essay tests on the lectures and a few papers liberally laced with and totally based on the authority of quotations. Nothing presented in class was ever questioned or discussed. Literature was studied as an intellectual discipline only, not as a living art for appreciation and enjoyment.

In a fair number of countries where English has the role of a foreign language, the treatment of literature in the classroom does not differ materially from what has been reported above. Possibly the two major differences concern the use of literature as material for mastery of the reading skill and an excessive devotion to translation as a classroom activity. With respect to the first, it is not unusual in many of the Asian countries, especially where English instruction begins as early as the elementary school, to use nursery rhymes and other simple material in the beginning grades, and also at a fairly early point to employ poetry as material for class or choral reading. In Indonesia, Masefield's "Sea Fever" and Blake's "Tiger" are reported as being so used. In many countries, as well, simplified or abridged versions of literary works are read, either all the way through secondary school or for the first half of it. Again, the purpose is the development of reading skill and the building up of vocabulary through the use of controlled materials.

The temptation to spend the major share of class time in translating literary selections from their original English to the native language appears to be overwhelming, and in some countries, at least, it seems difficult to persuade teachers that there can be any other form of class activity. Obviously, of course, with poetry this can amount to little more than paraphrase, but even where novels and short stories are given this kind of classroom treatment, it is likely to provide the student with an opportunity to develop his skill in the manipulation of his native language rather than the English that he is in class to learn. One hesitates to say so, but the reason for the popularity of translation as a class activity would seem to be that it demands the least of the teacher while at the same time it seems to furnish a fairly objective measure of the pupils' comprehension.

The reliance upon translation extends even into the upper reaches of the university curriculum. A native American member of the faculty of a private university in Japan writes, "The seminars seem glorified reading classes. They tend to cover one book per year per class. Per year! The main difference between seminars and lectures is the size. Lectures are bigger, and the teacher is expected to talk throughout. In the seminar there is a smaller class and more chance to ask the student to do something, though I take it the students are just asked questions of fact and to translate at random."

Gradually some American teachers in Japan have adopted the practice of raising questions of interpretation, of relevance, and of values, literary and ethical. The same teacher who was quoted in the foregoing paragraph continues:

In gathering this information I talked yesterday with some graduates, former students of mine. They said that in their college years only I had asked them their own opinion of the work under discussion. That was in a lecture class on drama. That lecture class has become a seminar and in the seminar (conducted in English) I do ask for opinions almost entirely, working with a modified Socratic method which I once thought impossible but which *can* be done. As I say, though, this is very unusual. Usually only the teacher talks.

It is somewhat more difficult to make valid generalizations about the nature of the literary materials which are taught and the principles of organization or presentation. The literary survey is rarely found below university level, and even there much of the curriculum is organized on a types and forms basis. There is no clear practice with respect to the place of American literature, except that dealing with it seperately is more likely to occur in university classes. An informant from Korea makes the interesting point that in the secondary schools there, much of the poetry was English and the bulk of the short stories were American.

With respect to the individual readings, one encounters some rather strange items which arouse one's curiosity about the principles or philosophy which serves as a criterion for selection: Bulfinch's *Tales of Ancient Gods and Heroes* cheek by jowl with Erich Fromm's *The Art of Loving*, both of them at least one remove from what might be considered authentic literary output in English. Unquestionably two factors do exercise some influence here, the age of the faculty and the availability and cost of the materials. For example, R. D. Blackmore's *Lorna Doone* and Anthony Hope's *Prisoner of Zenda* are reported as being on the eleventh and twelfth grade reading lists respectively in Thailand. Undoubtedly they were first put there by a person or persons who had read them at the time they appeared, or shortly after, and who accepted the contemporary overvaluation of them as literary works. It is possible also that since the copyright on them has long since expired, they may be reprinted without cost, whereas the royalties on recent works may be fairly high.

As we turn to situations where English has the role of a second language, we encounter, not unexpectedly, a longer period throughout which literature is dealt with in one form or another. Nursery rhymes and anecdotes about such American heroes as Washington and Lincoln are kindergarten and early elementary fare. Simplified versions of works such as *Robinson Crusoe*, *King Arthur and the Knights of the Round Table*, and even Washington Irving's *Alhambra* are introduced in the third and fourth grades.

Following a practice which has been mentioned in connection with secondary school curricula in the United States, the first three years seem to have been organized on the basis of themes which would reflect the maturing interests of the pupils, whereas the fourth year is a dual survey, first of British and then of American literature. Since the medium of instruction in most second-language countries is English, the tendency to spend long stretches of class time in translation seems not to arise. A good description of the nature and range of classroom activities is to be found in this statement from a Filipino teacher of English (personal communication).

> The teacher assigned you a selection, either in its entirety or only part of it. He first gave you questions for comprehension and vocabulary work. A student kept a vocabulary notebook which the teacher inspected regularly. Stories were for "reproducing" in class or in the form of written summary. Poetry was for explaining, paraphrasing, or interpreting. You kept a memory-gems notebook where you wrote down the lines you fancied most, including author and selection. A quota of two hundred lines was considered ideal. Essays were for making précis or translations, by a method we called "jumbling." This was Benjamin Franklin's method for self-improvement, a technique in writing where he first paraphrased a passage and then tried to rewrite it in the style of the original author. Plays were for discussion of moral implications and, of course, for dramatic reading. Longer works like novels and biographies formed the basis for home reading reports. The teacher gave you a list of titles and equivalent points to complete a reading quota.

From the description given, there appears to be little difference in the class activities and the concept of literary instructional aims from what one might have expected to encounter in a traditional presentation of the subject in the United States almost any time up to possibly 1940. It is quite possible that the winds of change abroad did not blow quite as early as they did on the American mainland.

The tendency of a country where English has a second-language status to model its English program after what prevails in the English-speaking nation with which it has the closest relationship is illustrated not only by the description of the program in the Philippines but by that followed in the British crown colony of Hong Kong as well. Both the Certificate of Education examination, advanced level, and the matriculation examination for the University of Hong Kong are modeled closely after their British counterparts. In fact, passes in the latter examination are accepted at some ten universities in the United Kingdom.

At the present time these examinations are an interesting mixture of the traditional and of more recent developments which recognize a considerable amount of contemporary literature. There are questions on Shakespeare appearing alongside topics based on John Wyndham, William Golding, Arthur Miller, and George Orwell. There are "period" questions, but the examiners no longer feel an obligation to include every period in the course of English literary history. In fact, the most recent advanced-level examination handbook offers the Augustan period and 1890–1930 as alternatives. Of the other two sections of the examination, one is given over to Shakespeare and the other is organized on a types and forms basis.

An informant from Hong Kong comments, "Compared with the curriculum in my day, there seems to have been a changed emphasis in materials. There is an attempt at cross-cultural understanding, as instanced by the Australian anthology. The syllabus is more student centered, contextually and experientially. It is also flexible and comprehensive in that the English Department works closely with the European Languages and Literatures Department, the Chinese Department, the Philosophy Department, the Psychology Department, and the English Language Center to facilitate the widest choice of study programs. Although there had been inter-departmental programs, they were not as activated and cooperative as they are now" (private communication).

Modern as this sounds, it is important to observe that one element is still lacking, that of breaking down the intensive preoccupation with English and American writing and moving toward a broadened concept of literature in English irrespective of country, and in the case of many of the ESL countries, the inclusion of writers past and present from that country. The mention of Australia by the Hong Kong informant is somewhat deceptive, since the anthology referred to consists mainly of English and American selections.

Unfortunately it is still a rarity for contemporary writers in the various ESL countries to be included in the curriculum. In fact, in some countries, notably India, there seems to be a strong feeling against it, irrationally enough, since it exists side by side with complaints about the lack of student interest in the conventional literary fare. The Oxford University Press has published a number of adventure stories with Asian and African settings, employing a controlled vocabulary. These, however, serve the purpose of skill builders in reading rather than literary texts.

There is very little to say about the countries where English has the status of a language of study, since a consideration of their specific needs has only really just begun. At present the English for Special Purposes usually takes the guise of a single course, divided into sections representing various subject-matter interests. Planning for and experience in meeting the professional needs of the students involved here has not yet reached a point where anything that is done goes beyond an ad hoc basis. I believe that there are possibilities which have not yet been sufficiently considered or explored. These will be discussed when the principles of curricular selection are dealt with.

CHAPTER 5

Factors Influencing
the Teaching of Literature
in the Foreign-Language
Curriculum

ALTHOUGH the role of the English language in a country and the effect of this upon educational aims, and the pedagogical tradition of the teaching of literature have been identified as the two principal influences upon the place and the teaching of English literature in the foreign-language or second-language curriculum, there are other factors as well which must be taken into consideration. The possible impact of four of these in particular merits some discussion: the availability of English literature translated into the native language; the relationship between the teaching of literature and the cultural objective in modern-language instruction; the peculiar problem posed by the English lexicon; questions about the use of abridged and simplified texts. These will be taken up in turn as subsections of the present chapter.

The Availability of English Literature in Translation

Some years ago the cultural attaché at the Italian embassy in Washington wrote and published a small pamphlet describing the contemporary literary scene in Italy. In it he commented that the then-current American concept of contemporary Italian literature was almost completely determined by the particular authors and works which had been translated; that it was quite different from the French view of Italian literature because a different assortment of literary fare had been translated into French, and that both of these differed materially from an Italian's view of his own literature which he, of course, was able to confront in its totality without translation. Even though we may concede that the teachers of English within a country are the ones who need translation the least, some of them may well be among the ranks of the translators and may even have a voice in deciding what is to be translated. At all events, literary translation is a part of the publishing business; it is expected to be reasonably profitable. As a result, the translated works of authors who write in English can serve as an index of what kind of literature is of interest to the reading public in that country, and moreover, if properly used, can constitute an effective teaching aid.

There would be little point in presenting here a detailed account of the extent of literary translations from English into as many other languages for which data might be secured, or even from a representative sampling of these countries. Besides, the situation is liable to change. At one time the American literary work which was available in translation in every German bookshop was Margaret Mitchell's *Gone with the Wind*. But this was twenty years ago. Undoubtedly its popularity has since been rivaled. Upon the occasion on my last visit to Poland, there seemed to be a recently developed rash of translations from James Fenimore Cooper. Such situations are undoubtedly ephemeral. For our purposes, more important than a detailed knowledge of the works and authors which have been translated in each country is an awareness of the entire range of questions about translation which ought to be asked, and the implications for the teaching of English literature that might be drawn from the answers.

Not only is it important to know something about the quantity of literature originally written in English that is available in a country, but it is equally desirable to form some impression as to how available it is. There is clearly a significant difference between wide distribution in inexpensive paperbound editions hawked on the street and available for purchase at every kind of little shop, on the one hand, and limited availability in expensively printed and bound editions, on the other. Another factor to be considered here is, in the event that the country is multilingual, into which of the various native languages have English literary works been translated, or have they been translated into what serves the country as a second language but into none of the native languages, as might be the case in Francophone Africa? The answers to these questions will help to define the sectors of the public which are open to some literary and cultural interchange with the various English-speaking nations.

Before one considers specific authors and works, certain questions of broader scope arise. The first of these is whether or not the literature that is translated is chiefly contemporary or from the older periods. The plays of Shakespeare seem to have had a host of translators the world over, many of them extremely able and distinguished. But even the Old English epic *Beowulf* has been translated into a surprising number of languages, most of them Western European, to be sure. The question about the modernity of the works translated can become important in a period when literary styles and values seem to reflect a pronounced change in taste and interest.

In the case of literature written in English, it is important to know whether British or American authors are more heavily represented in the works which are translated. And naturally one would want to know whether writers in English other than British or American have attracted the public interest. Another telling index of public interest is to be found in the genre of the works that are most frequently translated: whether they are novels, short stories, poems, plays, or essays. At times the popularity of certain literary genres in translation would seem to be affected by what is available in the native literature. For example, the nineteenth-century German novella, despite its excellence, never seemed to excite much interest in the United States, possibly because of the excellent craftsmanship of the short stories produced in this country.

One turns from these questions of general import to the consideration of particular authors and specific works which would seem to have captivated public interest. It is rare for the complete works of an author to be translated, except in the case of Shakespeare in some countries. But again this is fortunate in a sense: to know that in a particular country Sinclair Lewis's *Babbitt* has been translated but not his *Arrowsmith* would seem to suggest something about the nature of the life problems and literary themes which will interest the reading public there.

Plays have a second dimension of interest because, after all, they are written to be performed. A translated play can be most successful on the stage. During the theatrical season of 1953–1954, without question the most popular play on the German and Austrian stages was a translation of Thornton Wilder's *Our Town*. Other questions arise here as well; one of them is whether the plays are performed by amateur or professional companies. This might have a bearing on whether a particular play has something of a cult interest or a broad general appeal. The nature of the audience is of some importance in this connection—as it is, in fact, in considering the entire translation question, or possibly in this context one should say readership.

Thus far we have dealt primarily with quantitative aspects of translation: how many works, from which parts of the English-speaking world, which authors, which books? There is also a qualitative dimension to be considered. How successfully is the translation able to put into the native language not only the letter but the spirit of the work which is being translated? Investigations into this question as it applies to specific works may prove to be most enlightening to teachers, may have an important bearing on the works selected for study, and may throw into sharp focus the cultural characteristics of the literature.

In those countries where translation of the literary work from English into the language of instruction constitutes the bulk of the classroom activity, it will be hard for teachers to conceive of the possibility of using translations as teaching aids. In fact, I have been told by some teachers that they keep abreast of the native translations of English literary works in order to know what *not* to teach, namely the works that have been translated. This would seem to be a self-defeating attitude. Certainly, one of the many difficulties imposed by an adherence to translation as the primary classroom activity is the sheer tediousness of doing the same thing day after day, combined with the length of time required to cover a work even of moderate length in this manner. This applies to novels and full-length plays in particular. If, instead of plodding through the entire work as class translation, four or five key episodes or chapters, those upon which the entire work seems to turn, were selected for this kind of treatment, and the rest were covered by rapid reading in the native language, more of the literature could be covered in a less tiresome fashion, to the increased satisfaction of at least the students, if not the teacher.

In conclusion, it is worth repeating that the primary purpose here has been to call attention to the role that translations of English literature can play in the development and determination of the literary curriculum and in modifying classroom procedures—a matter that has rarely been explored in treatments of foreign-language or second-language teaching. It is something which simply has to be dealt with on an individual country-by-country basis, primarily because no general conclusions are possible. The extent of translation varies from almost nothing in Malaysia to almost everything in Japan; also from an almost exclusive concern with modern literature in some countries to a full chronological range in others, from a heavy concentration on American writers in some countries to their relative exclusion in others. Under these circumstances, generalizations are difficult, if not impossible. The attempt here has been primarily to suggest the questions that ought to be asked.

The Cultural Component in the Literary Curriculum

Implicit in the article by Dr. Thelma Kintanar referred to in the first chapter of this study, "The Role of Literature in Culture Learning" (1972), was the assumption that literature does have a role, irrespective of what particular concept of culture one accepts. Let us begin our consideration of this topic by raising certain problems of cultural interpretation in terms of specific literary selections and then move on to the larger question of the extent of the cultural impact that one may reasonably expect from literature in another country and another culture.

Admittedly all truly great literature deals with the universals of human experience, and so does much that might be placed in the "good but not truly great" category. Yet the particular events and emotions depicted in the literature are often very strongly tied to the culturally determined or conditioned outlook of the writer. To take a simple example, marriage is common to most societies, but the arrangements and the implications of both the ceremony and the entire relationship will be as varied as the societies in which they occur. For example, a domestic scene in an American short story, portraying a young couple doing the household chores together with newly married affection, would not arouse the admiration its author intended in any number of other cultures, where a husband wearing an apron and helping in the kitchen would be considered an affront to manhood rather than a token of generous love.

One kind of difficulty can arise when the teacher is so completely a product of the author's culture that he is unaware of any cultural issues that a selection might raise. An American teacher might consider Robert Frost's contention, "something there is that doesn't love a wall," to be a credible, even an admirable point of view, not realizing that in certain cultures the concept of unmarked property boundaries is completely unthinkable and will strike the foreign teacher of English as well as the student in precisely the same manner. Indeed, this very issue has arisen in Germany, in a slightly altered form, namely that of closed or open doors to executive offices of large American firms headquartered there. The Germans want to close their office doors; the Americans want to keep theirs open. To the latter, the closed door seems inhospitable if not conspiratorial; to the former the open door seems messy and unbusinesslike.

Another kind of problem occurs where there is no cultural equivalent of what is being portrayed in the literature. This might well be the case in many countries with the particular form the Christmas legend takes in such a poem as Thomas Hardy's "The Oxen." In such instances, all that is required, or indeed all that can be done, is an explanation by the teacher designed to supply the necessary cultural context.

The most serious difficulties come about when similar objects, actions, or points of view have one set of values in the student's culture and a quite different one in the English-speaking audience for whom the author was writing. "The Sculptor's Funeral," by Willa Cather, is a short story which deals with the funeral, in his small-town midwestern native home, of a famous sculptor who has become completely alienated from his early environment. One incident portrays the mother, essentially a mean-spirited woman, indulging in unrestrained grief as her son's body is brought into the room. The author is suggesting that the mother's behavior is wholly hypocritical, and she clearly intended her readers to be repelled by it. Yet the behavior in question would be regarded as both natural and expected in many cultures. The same is true of the living room decor in the Merrick family home, intended by the author as a horrible example of bad taste, but there is no assurance that it will be so interpreted in many countries.

It is not always easy, especially for a nonnative teacher, to determine the implicit attitudes and values of the students in his classroom. Yet the answers to questions like, "Would you expect to find something like this here?" or "Would someone do this in your country?" can be revealing and useful. They not only encourage a student to extend his vocabulary by expressing ideas that are familiar to him, but also make it possible to determine whether he understands the values and assumptions that are implicit in the literary selection. To teach literature is, in effect, to teach that part of the culture upon which the writing is based. It is a by-product rather than the principal purpose; the latter being that of sharing the literary experience. Nevertheless, culture has an important role to play.

This leads to the question, what, precisely, is the nature of that role? I believe that this question can best be discussed from the vantage point of a situation where English has the role of a second language, or at least we may begin there. In such countries, bilingualism for either all or a significant sector of the population is the professed goal of the educational process. This raises the issue whether the acquisition of a considerable degree of competence in the language should imply the acquisition of a second culture as well. This is an interesting and yet a difficult question.

Throughout the course of a full academic life with fairly extensive foreign contacts, I have come to know a number of persons who, if not bilingual to the point that neither language could be considered dominant, yet were highly competent in two languages. I doubt that any one of them could realistically be described as bicultural. In fact, I have known some bilinguals who were partially alienated from both their mother-country culture and their second or acquired one. There is no question but that biculturalism is a very complex matter, but I believe that one can arrive at a reasonable educational objective with respect to it.

In order to do so, one must begin with language and take cognizance of the distinction between a receptive and a productive command of a second language. There is generally a considerable gap between the two: we comprehend more than we can say or write. Even in our native language, we recognize many words when we hear them or come upon them in print, though we do not use them ourselves. In my own case, I have been aware of the verb *fetch* ever since I was a child, ever since I first heard the nursery rhyme "Jack and Jill," yet I doubt that I have productively used it in the course of a long life. Various uses of *bring, take*, and *get* function in its place. Recently sports broadcasters have taken to using the term *zip* for 'zero' or 'nothing' in reporting game scores. I recognize it; I cannot imagine myself using it. On a somewhat different level, I would never use the term *folks* to apply either to relatives or to associates, yet it occurs commonly in the speech of certain good friends. I understand *effectuate* in the sense of 'to bring about', but I consider the term a repulsive example of bureaucratic jargon and shy away from it. I am reasonably confident that my experience and practice here would find their counterparts in other native speakers. It has been estimated by some that among speakers of English the receptive vocabulary is possibly three times as large as the productive vocabulary.

This leads one to wonder if an equally valid distinction between reception and production might not be made with respect to culture. Can we not assume a situation where a person realizes that there are characteristic modes of behavior, attitudes, and values which, when he encounters them in someone else, he will recognize not as personal idiosyncracies but as manifestations of a shared behavior; he recognizes them for what they are but would probably not adopt them. For example, Europeans and Americans manipulate their dinner forks in totally different ways. When almost any American first sees someone use his fork in a European manner, he is likely to be repelled at the sight. Sooner or later, if his transatlantic contacts continue, he will in all probability come to accept it as a culture trait. Only in the most extreme situation would he be likely to adopt it, although every consideration of ease and efficiency would seem to recommend it. To take just another brief illustration, for many peoples of the world, most Americans among them, the initial meal of the day is one in which the menu is not likely to be matched or repeated by any other meal. For countless others, no such distinction is made between breakfast and whatever other meals may follow. Several months or years of life in Mexico may accustom someone from the United States to seeing the natives consume a *desayuno* consisting of frijoles refritos and Coca Cola, possibly laced with a bit of tequila, but again it is not a practice which he is likely to adopt.

These illustrations have all been on a somewhat rudimentary level, but I believe they illustrate the distinction between perceiving and understanding a culturally governed action on the one hand, and acting upon it on the other. Could we not, then, apply this to the question of the cultural component in literature, and by extension, accept it as an educational goal for a country in which English has the role of a second language? Stated briefly, it would be that manifestations of the culture of one or more of the English-speaking nations be recognized for what they are; that the usual instant visceral and hostile reactions to them be overcome, but that Anglo-Saxon values and modes of behavior should not necessarily serve as models for imitation. Naturally, this will have some implications for the kind of literature selected for study and for the mode of presenting it. Certainly, it is educationally sounder to recognize the cultural factor and to attempt to deal with it in terms of some kind of policy than it would be to ignore it.

Thus far the problem has been considered primarily from the point of view of a country where English has the role of a second language. Naturally some kind of cross-cultural understanding is vital in order for the second language to exercise its social function. But it will be understanding rather than adoption of the second culture which will prevail. Filipino rhetoric will remain just that, with its high valuation of a somewhat ornate vocabulary. It will not be stripped to the naked economy of what many college English instructors in the United States consider to be in the best tradition of Anglo-Saxon prose.

If the restricted aim of cultural understanding is what we may justifiably hope for in a second-language situation, obviously we cannot look for more in those countries where English has a less pervasive role, that of a foreign language. On the other hand, among the various aims of modern language instruction in such a country, the cultural component is probably of heightened relative importance. By all means the most important thing to remember is that cultural awareness, sensitivity, and rapprochement are not automatic by-products of foreign-language instruction or of exposure to a foreign literature. If they are to be achieved at all, they must be planned for and built into the course of study.

This is not likely to be accomplished by lectures dealing directly with the topic of the foreign culture. Nor will it be brought about by readings which deal with the question solely from a sociological or an anthropological viewpoint. Without question the most effective presentation will be through observing people in contexts, in situations where they act and react to each other in terms of their culture. Conformities to the native pattern may be just as significant as departures from it. Certainly a convenient source of material for observation is that of characters in literature, revealing not merely their actions but their thoughts and emotions as well, in a form which permits repeated impact and careful analysis.

The Vocabulary Problem

Vocabulary looms large in any consideration of teaching literature; it is probably more prominent than it deserves to be. This is partly the case because there are a number of widely held misconceptions about the English lexicon; consequently, it is worth the space and effort to correct as many of the erroneous notions as possible.

As languages go, English seems to have a very large vocabulary. Such full or unabridged dictionaries as the Oxford and the Webster's *New International* have approximately 500,000 entries, but in reality this is only a beginning as far as the totality of the language is concerned. Terms for the various species of insects and those for aniline dyes each run into the thousands, and these represent only two fairly specific areas of the vocabulary out of hundreds. At one time there was an American saying to the effect that "if it isn't in the dictionary, it isn't a word." In the light of what has just been said, this is clearly an untenable position, illustrating little or nothing more than the American cultural tendency, going back many decades, to grant a far greater degree of authority to the dictionary than the facts of lexicography warrant.

One consequence of this extraordinary word stock is that no single person commands more than a small fraction of the entire English lexicon. Precisely what "possessing" or "controlling" a word means is a moot point, but we generally estimate the recognition vocabulary of a child entering school at about 5,000 words. We also assume an increase of approximately 1,000 words annually. At this rate, by the age of eighteen—or the completion of secondary education—he should have some 17,000 or 18,000; by the age of twenty-two, the time of graduation from college, from 22,000 to 24,000. Persons engaged in intellectual pursuits, either vocationally or avocationally, attain a vocabulary of some 60,000. The productive vocabulary may amount to a third of these figures. Nevertheless, the original point remains. Even 60,000 is only some twelve percent of half a million, and what makes the matter even more difficult is that not everyone's twelve percent will consist of the same words.

Not only is the word stock of the language excessively large but it is highly composite as well. This has come about as a result of the position that the English language occupied at one or more points in its history, namely that of a substratum language. During the period of the Scandinavian invasions of England and especially in the tenth century, there was a considerable amount of linguistic give and take; many words of Norse origin found their way into the vocabulary. After the Norman Conquest and continuing for centuries, there was a constant heavy influx of words of French origin. The New Humanism of the Renaissance, with its rediscovery of the classics, provided a channel for the entry of words of Latin and Greek origin. The extension of the English language to all parts of the globe by Queen Elizabeth's intrepid explorers and the colonizers who followed them has resulted in the introduction into the vocabulary of words from almost every conceivable source, from Eskimo-Aleut to Malay. Moreover, English seems to have preferred to borrow words instead of meeting the challenge posed by new movements, concepts, and environments by fashioning words for them out of elements already existing within the language.

In addition to the difficulties imposed by the composite and gargantuan vocabulary, we must recognize another aspect of the problem, this one arising from the facts of word distribution. In considering the matter, it is necessary first of all to make a distinction between word 'types' and word 'tokens'. By a type, we mean a word as such; by a token we refer to an individual or single occurrence of a word. Thus in the sentence immediately preceding this, there are two tokens each for the word types *word*, *by*, and *we*.

There are two aspects of word distribution which bear upon language-teaching activities and especially upon the reading of literature. First, a selection of possibly 5,000 words, that is to say tokens, in length may well have about 1,000 word types. Of these 1,000, roughly half will occur in the passage only once; possibly 250 will appear twice, and another 125 three times. At this point we have already accounted for 875 types, seven-eighths of the 1,000 total. They consist of words which will not occur often enough to serve as memory reinforcement. They are also words which the student may not come upon again in any other reading that he does.

There is a second strange element in the distribution as well. In the foregoing paragraph we considered the difficulties arising from the vast number of words which appear only infrequently. There is, in addition, a very small number of words which appear with great frequency. In any passage with normal word distribution, perhaps no more than 50 word types will be represented by sixty to seventy percent of the word tokens. For the most part these high-frequency items are not content words; they exercise grammatical functions of one sort or another. Included among them are the definite and indefinite articles, personal pronouns, prepositions, conjunctions, forms of the verb *to be*. In one word count of the English language, it is the twenty-sixth word in order of frequency that is the first to have a referential or lexical meaning; the preceding twenty-five are all part of the grammatical mechanism of the language.

It is easy to see what kind of pedagogical problem this creates, especially in connection with the reading of literature where the vocabulary has not been tampered with or simplified. Clearly, an uncomfortably large proportion of words will occur only in a single selection, not in the next which the pupil will encounter, nor in the one after that. Memorizing long lists of words which occur only once is neither a pleasant nor a satisfactory approach to the problem, nor is the burdensome task of consulting the dictionary for every unrecognized lexical item. Although replicating the process of native-language learning is anything but an infallible guide in dealing with foreign-language learning problems, it is worth considering in this connection. Although not everyone learns new vocabulary items in the same manner, and these differences in learning styles must be taken into account, most of us acquire new words in our receptive vocabularies by adducing their meanings from the contexts in which they occur. Repeated exposure, where the word occurs in slightly different contexts, fleshes out its meaning and also prepares one to use it if the opportunity presents itself.

To illustrate with a concrete example, most newcomers to Hawaii will first encounter the loanword *kokua* from the newspaper column, *The Kokua Line*, which will be a parallel to the title *The Action Line* in the newspapers on the mainland. There is a very good chance that the word will next be encountered on a poster inside a municipal bus, asking the passengers to refrain from smoking, eating, or playing radios. Here the word appears in a parallel construction with *please* and *mahalo*, the latter another borrowing meaning 'thank you'. This muddies the waters a bit since one cannot be certain which of the other two items to equate it with—or neither. Next, it may be encountered as a verb in a news story, reporting someone as saying, "I'll kokua," suggesting something like agreement with subsequent action. This is still fumbling, perhaps, but nevertheless the semantic range of the word is beginning to be rounded out. Notice that this particular example has a dual usefulness: it tells us something about the way in which the borrowing process goes on and also something about the normal way in which most of us acquire new vocabulary.

It has already been suggested that there are three possible ways of coping with the vocabulary problem: memorizing vocabulary lists, consulting a dictionary for every word which is not known, and determining insofar as possible the meaning of new vocabulary items from context. Given the facts about the size of the English lexicon and about word distribution, the first is doomed to futility. The second is an invitation to boredom. It is only the third which has in itself the potential for continued growth and flexibility.

There are certain other measures which may be of material assistance in dealing with problems of the lexicon. One is a study of derivative prefixes and suffixes, and the modifications in meaning which they exercise when they are added to base forms. If a pupil recognizes an English verb most of the time when he encounters one, and if he also knows that the suffix -er, when added to the base form of the verb, makes an agent noun out of it (think, thinker), he has in effect increased his receptive vocabulary by a number equivalent to the number of verbs he already knows. The same would be true for such other high-frequency suffixes as -ness and for prefixes such as re- and un-, to mention only a few.

With certain languages the recognition of cognate forms can be very helpful in vocabulary increase. This is true chiefly of the Germanic and the Romance languages, the first serving as the principal base of the English lexicon and the second accounting for the major share of foreign borrowings. Outside of this sphere they are not likely to be helpful unless, as in the case of the Philippines, Francophone Africa, and certain Caribbean islands, there is a fairly wide knowledge of either a Romance or of a Germanic language. There is also some danger here because of the lack of exact equivalence in meaning in cognate pairs: mistaking French *demander* for English 'demand' rather than 'ask' may lead, as it has in the past, to strained relationships. Even the difference between Spanish *educacion*, 'breeding, rearing', and English *education* may produce misunderstandings.

Despite the reservations expressed here about the use of dictionaries, naturally they cannot be dispensed with entirely, but it is most important to guard against the incorrect impressions and misinformation they may convey. This is most likely to result from the use of greatly condensed bilingual dictionaries, where for the most part a single word equivalent in the target language is supplied for each entry in the native. This is not only inadequate but can be positively misleading, as for example when the English verb *trim* is glossed only by a word or expressing meaning 'to cut close' and not also by one meaning 'to adorn, embellish'. It is far preferable to use a dictionary which explains the meanings of English words in English, and some good ones are widely available.

Reduced and Abridged Texts

Simplified or condensed versions of literary texts are at least as old as Lamb's *Tales from Shakespeare*, which goes back about a century and a half. In this instance there is also a change of genre, from drama to prose narrative, as well as simplification. Within the English-speaking countries, *Robinson Crusoe*, *Gulliver's Travels*, and *Uncle Tom's Cabin* are frequently published in simplified form because of their story appeal to children, although no one of them was intended as a children's book. In a sense, therefore, we are not dealing with anything new.

Generally speaking, texts are simplified in response to one of two motives. Sometimes both of them enter into the situation. First, there may be the desire to recast the selection, using words and constructions that can be understood by a child or by a nonnative speaker who has not fully mastered the language. Treatment of this kind may not necessarily shorten the work; in fact it could conceivably maintain the original length or even lengthen it.

Today, this aim is usually achieved by the imposition of strict vocabulary controls, determined on a word-frequency basis, For a time, some three decades ago, much literature was rewritten in Basic English, also a limited vocabulary but based upon considerations other than word frequency. For the most part, very little has been done with the grading of syntactic structures on the basis of relative difficulty, although this would seem to be quite as important as vocabulary control.

The second type of treatment falling into the categories which are being considered here might best be termed an abridgment. Its purpose is to reduce the length, and accordingly the reading time, of a long selection for the purpose of eliminating the fatigue and boredom which is bound to set in if the class treatment of a literary piece stretches over weeks and months. This would apply particularly to those classes where the principal, if not the sole, activity consists of word-for-word and line-by-line translation.

In connection with both of these types of reduction, the important question is how the text has been affected by the operation. Has it been damaged or weakened? Has it been improved? Naturally, opinions vary on this point. Nelson Brooks characterizes simplification as an "act that does unwonted violence to the author's intent and lulls the reader into a false sense of security" (1960, p. 101). On the other hand, publishers continue to publish them, which seems to imply that teachers continue to use them. There would seem to be only one way to deal with this problem here, and that is to compare some of these versions with their originals, and on the basis of this comparison, to arrive at whatever conclusions are possible. Naturally the limitations of space will not permit an extended or in-depth comparison, but there is something to be gained from even a casual examination.

In 1962, Edith Fries Croft and Kenneth Croft adapted for class use four of Jack London's best-known stories of the Far North. In their introduction they claim to have shortened the stories, but in the case of the one which is to be examined here, this is not true. The adaptations may be a little longer than the originals. At best, they are of equal length. The Crofts also assert (p. viii) that "vocabulary control has been applied: the stories have been rewritten within a 3000-item word list (A *General Service List of English Words*, edited by Michael West, supplemented by the Thorndike list to number 30): when other vocabulary appears, footnote explanations, and, in a few instances, pictured illustrations are given."

The second story in the volume has the title "Journey for What?" and is divided into three segments of seven to ten octavo pages each, to facilitate class treatment. An adaptation of a story which its author originally called "The Sun-dog Trail," it originally appeared in *Harper's Monthly Magazine* in 1905. A comparison of the first two paragraphs of the adaptation with the first two paragraphs of the original is admittedly a highly restricted sample, but it does serve to reveal some interesting facets of the adaptation process. For the sake of convenience in referring to them, the sentences of the original have been numbered.

Original:

THE SUN-DOG TRAIL

(1) Sitka Charley smoked his pipe and gazed thoughtfully at the newspaper illustration on the wall. (2) For half an hour he had been steadily regarding it, and for half an hour I had been slyly watching him. (3) Something was going on in that mind of his, and, whatever it was, I knew it was well worth knowing. (4) He had lived life, and seen things, and performed that prodigy of prodigies, namely, the turning of his back upon his own people, and, in so far as it was possible for an Indian, becoming a white man even in his mental processes. (5) As he phrased it himself, he had come into the warm, sat among us, by our fires, and become one of us.

(6) We had struck this deserted cabin after a hard day on trail. (7) The dogs had been fed, the supper dishes washed, the beds made, and we were now enjoying that most delicious hour that comes each day, on the Alaskan trail, when nothing intervenes between the tired body and bed save the smoking of the evening pipe.

Adaptation:

JOURNEY FOR WHAT?

Sitka Charley smoked his pipe and gazed thoughtfully at a picture from a magazine which someone had fastened to the wall. For half an hour he had been looking at it steadily, and for half an hour I had been watching him secretly. He was thinking about something, and whatever it was, it was well worth knowing about. He had lived many years, seen many things, and had done one thing that was particularly unusual. He had left his own people—the Indians—and, in so far as it was possible for an Indian, had become a white man, even in his mental processes. As he expressed it himself: he had come out of the cold, sat among us by our fires, and become one of us. He had never learned to read or write, but his vocabulary was remarkable. And more remarkable still was the completeness with which he had adopted the white man's attitude toward everything.

We had found this deserted cabin after a hard day's travel. The dogs had been fed, the supper dishes washed, the beds made; and we were now enjoying that most delightful hour that comes each day—and only once each day on the Alaskan trail—the hour when nothing stands between the tired body and bed expect the smoking of the evening pipe.

In comparing the two, the first thing to note is that the previous statement to the effect that an adaptation may be longer than the original is amply borne out. The 121 words in the first paragraph of the original are expanded to 158 in the adaptation; the figures for the second are 57 and 63 respectively.

Beyond the matter of sheer length, the first thing that catches one's attention is the change in title. *Sun-dog*, a term for a parahelion or halo, is probably not familiar to many native speakers of English, so the motive for the change is easily understood, although for anyone who does know the term, a concrete image is lost. The first sentence in the adaptation is longer than the original, as a result of the change of the final phrase to a clause, although lexical simplicity is gained by substituting *picture* for *illustration*. It is difficult to understand why the adapters retained *gazed*, which is certainly not a high-frequency word—particularly in the light of their alteration of *regarding* to *looking at*. For reasons not wholly clear, the two adverbs have been shifted from the middle of the verb phrase to postverbal position. The passive construction of the first part of (3) is changed to active, and it is quite possible that the direct statement is easier to understand. *Slyly* in the original has been changed to *secretly*, very likely for reasons of frequency, although they do not have the same connotation. *He* in the next sentence makes a personal active subject out of what was impersonal and passive. The fourth sentence in the original becomes two in the adaptation, with a considerable simplification of vocabulary as well as structure, although with an increase in the total wordage. Finally, the first paragraph ends with two explanatory sentences which are not in the original at all—at least in the version which the Crofts profess to be the source of the adaptation.

The second paragraph understandably substitutes *found* for *struck*, *travel* for *on trail*, *delightful* for *delicious*, *stands between* for *intervenes*, *except* for *save*, and again a repetitive phrase is inserted.

Without question, some qualities are lost in the process of simplification, but possibly they would not have made an impact upon the nonnative reader in any event. Despite Charley's having become white in his mental processes, London leaves him with a few telltale markers of the non-Anglo in his speech. In referring to a child in a picture, Charley asks, "The little girl—does it die?" The adaptation changes this to the conventional *she*. The original abounds in noncontracted verb forms; the adaptation collapses them into contracted forms, possibly to fit a concept of easy, casual speech. But the retention of the full forms would not necessarily be at all unnatural for a nonnative speaker, which may have been what London wanted to suggest.

The title of the adaptation, "Journey for What?" does bring out the mystery or lack of meaning of the principal narrative to a degree that the title of the original does not. Yet in focusing so specifically upon the incident itself, the adaptation runs the risk of detracting attention from the larger meaning, namely that slices of life do not always have a recognizable beginning and end, and that consequently their significance may be hard to isolate or recognize. Nonetheless it must be conceded that the adaptation does maintain a high degree of fidelity to the original, though not without some loss of flavor. It does succeed in easing the reading difficulty to some degree, but as we have seen, there is no reduction in length.

It is not easy to decide if the gain in using the adaptation will outweigh the loss, and probably no hard and fast rule will fit all conceivable circumstances. The kind of comparison which has been briefly undertaken here should, however, serve as an illustration of the in-depth study that should be entered upon whenever the question of the possible use of an adaptation is up for consideration. It is, moreover, an exercise that is quite within the competence of the teacher as well as the supervisor or curriculum specialist and should be profitable for anyone who engages in it.

We turn now from the adaptation to the abridgment, again selecting a typical example for comparison with the original, in this instance a reduction of *The Invisible Man*, by H. G. Wells (Williams 1959). Wells was one of the first writers of what might be called science fiction. This particular narrative could be classified as a short novel or a long short story. The abridged version represents a reduction to two-thirds the length of the original and a simplification to the level of the 2,000 words of Michael West's *A General Service List*. The illustrative examples cited here are drawn from the very beginning of the story.

Original:

MR. TEDDY HENFREY'S FIRST IMPRESSION

At Gleeson's corner he saw Hall, who had recently married the stranger's hostess at the "Coach and Horses," and who now drove the Ipping conveyance, when occasional people required it, to Sidderbridge Junction, coming towards him on his return from that place. Hall had evidently been "stopping a bit" at Sidderbridge, to judge by his driving. " 'Ow do, Teddy?" he said, passing.

"You got a rum un up home!" said Teddy.

Hall very sociably pulled up. "What's that?" he asked.

"Rum-looking customer stopping at the 'Coach and Horses,' " said Teddy. "My sakes!"

And he proceeded to give Hall a vivid description of his wife's grotesque guest. "Looks a bit like a disguise, don't it? I'd like to see a man's face if I had him stopping in *my* place," said Henfrey. "But women are that trustful—where strangers are concerned. He's took your rooms, and he ain't even given a name, Hall."

Abridgment:

FIRST IMPRESSIONS

At the street corner he saw Hall, who had lately married the lady of the inn. "How do, Teddy?" said Hall as he passed.

"You've got a strange visitor!" said Teddy.

Hall stopped. "What's that?" he asked.

"Queer man stopping at the inn," said Teddy.

And he described Mrs. Hall's guest. "Looks a bit funny, doesn't it? I'd like to see a man's face if I had him stopping in *my* house," said Henfrey. "But women are so simple with strangers. He's taken your rooms, and he hasn't even given a name."

The first thing to observe is that the 153 words of the original have been reduced to 92 in the abridgment, thus maintaining roughly the one-third scale of reduction which was mentioned earlier. What is most surprising about this is that upon casually reading the two versions, the scale of reduction seems rather more drastic than the figure given. This impression probably derives from the fact that the passages of direct quotation, though often reworded, are about the same length as the original, unless they are omitted altogether. This leaves the burden of reduction to fall primarily upon the descriptive and narrative passages, especially the former.

As an illustration of the previous point, the 62 words of the first paragraph in Wells's original are cut to 24. The result is a loss of virtually all concrete, descriptive detail, and a reduction to whatever bare statements are necessary to keep the narrative moving. The treatment of the directly quoted passages is notable chiefly for the elimination of all dialect forms, those which might be considered local, and the rather more general markers of social dialect. Cockney *'ow*, the expression *rum un*, *took* used as a past participle, and *ain't* are all changed, laundered so to speak. The very specific "looks like a disguise" becomes "looks funny." The first sentence of the final paragraph again illustrates drastic reduction of descriptive language.

In short, what is lost in the abridgment is specifying detail, nonstandard language which can be helpful in characterizing a speaker, and also (though not illustrated in the specimens quoted above) passages which serve to indicate connection and sequence. One seems to have the bones of a skeleton rather than a fleshed-out body. The gain is in the ease of reading and the speed of getting through the selection.

These comparisons have been made not for the purpose of putting the simplified and abridged versions in an unfavorable light but rather to try to show what is lost and what may be gained in them. If unintentionally the approach here has seemed to be somewhat negative, it is only because what has been excised or changed shows up very concretely, whereas the gains can only be surmised.

With all due respect to Nelson Brooks, whose disapproval of simplified texts was quoted earlier in this section, the question of using or not using these altered versions is not just a simple matter of choosing up sides, of being for or against. To begin with, no two simplified versions will bear the same relationship to the original. As I have already suggested, in order to arrive at an evaluation of a simplified version, the kinds of comparison with the originals which have been illustrated here are absolutely necessary, except of course that they must be carried out on a far more extensive scale. Texts can be sampled, but the samples must be systematically selected in order to insure valid representation; the sampling can be undertaken by a group as well as an individual, but the point is that it should be done.

There are other factors which must also be considered in evaluating simplified texts. Important among these is a clear idea of the purpose of the particular selection at the point in the curriculum at which it has been placed. Is it merely to tell a story? Is it to present a concept of character and of character development? Is it to communicate a sense of setting, an atmosphere? If narrative interest is the principal element, and if the simplified version still tells a coherent story, the use of such a version may be defensible. If the interest goes beyond that, the gains must be weighed against the losses. In short, such a decision must be made in the light of a full and an impartial examination of as many of the pertinent factors as is possible.

CHAPTER 6

What Literature
To Teach:
Principles
of Selection
and Class Treatment

THE FOREGOING CHAPTERS have been devoted first to identifying and considering the issues relative to the inclusion of literature in the foreign-language or second-language curriculum, and subsequently to discussing the bearing of certain factors upon the problem. The latter has, upon occasion, drawn us somewhat far afield from the literature classroom. At this point, however, we are ready to return to our original concern and to conclude, not necessarily with a specific program, naming books and authors, but rather with a set of defensible principles which may be broadly applied.

We must recognize, first of all, that the sheer mass of literature produced in any one language spoken by tens, and in some instances hundreds, of millions of people is likely to be so vast that it defies the imagination. This is especially true when the country in question has a literary tradition that goes back some twelve centuries, as is the case with England. If one adds to that the literature which is produced in some eight or ten other English-speaking countries, the total is overwhelming.

What this means, of course, is that only a minute portion of the totality of literature in English can be studied in connection with any course or curriculum in English, whether as a native or as a second or foreign language. It means, as well, that there can be no fixed or set anthology, be it ten or a hundred best books of English literature that everyone is supposed to have read. For a novel by Dickens, one can with equal justice and conviction advocate one by Thackeray. Who will decide between the Pardoner's Tale and that by Chaucer's Prioress? Each is a gem of its own kind. This means, in effect, that the relatively small part of the literature that can be included in any curriculum must be chosen on the basis of some clearly defined principle or principles. The question then becomes, how do we arrive at them?

We must begin, I believe, with the general aims of the country's system of education (what kind of person and society is it geared to produce?) and proceed from there to the function of foreign or second language study and teaching within the system.

One way of viewing the function of education within a society is as a means of transmitting and perpetuating the traditional values, mores, attitudes, the lore and the credos of that society. For a long time the function of one important sector of British education, the public (in the British sense) schools and the university, was to turn out an English gentleman. At one time, and possibly still, the goal of American publicly supported education was to produce a participating citizen in a democracy. Goals such as these are defensible to a point, but there are certain dangers inherent in them as well. If the tradition, the lore, and the credos become too widely separated from the realities of life, there is a danger of creating a mandarin class, or of having the student reject what the educational system has to offer. This can also occur when the educational system transmits the traditions and values of only a single segment of the society, an aristocracy or a middle class let us say, to the exclusion of others.

There is another view of education that is particularly applicable to any country which professes to be a democracy. It puts the principal emphasis upon developing in every potential citizen the ability and the desire to think for himself, to question decisions no matter who makes them, and to maintain a skeptical attitude toward all information that comes to him through official channels, or unofficial ones for that matter. This view rests upon the premise that no society is perfect and that improvement in it can come only through trenchant criticism and a constant flow and free play of ideas. The purpose of the educational system becomes one of preparing the pupils for this task of the trenchant critic. This is the idea behind a book written not so long ago for English teachers by Neil Postman and Charles Weingartner: *Teaching as a Subversive Activity* (1969). The authors feel that subversion, in the sense in which they use the term, is the only path to the improvement of society. The same idea also lies behind a recently appointed committee of the National Council of Teachers of English, the Committee on Public Doublespeak. The function of this group is to expose semantic trickery in the public statements of government officials, the communications industry

—particularly in advertising—and big business, and to develop a sensitivity to such deceit, in the hope that this sensitivity will be passed on to the pupils. It has recently taken to awarding an annual mock prize to the public official responsible for the most obfuscating statement of the year. The winner in 1974 was Ronald Ziegler, the press secretary of former President Nixon.

It will be realized, of course, that the activities and the attitudes just described would be unthinkable in a dictatorship of any sort, whether of the left or the right. In the Marxist countries they would undoubtedly be attacked as "revisionist doctrine." A right-wing government would characterize them as unpatriotic, if not decadent. It should be remembered that when the National Socialist party came to power in Germany, the long-standing ideals of freedom to learn and freedom to teach were swiftly suppressed.

Even in a country such as the United States, where there is at least a technical commitment to freedom of thought and expression, this concept of the goals of education often runs into difficulties because the values and outlook of the intellectual sector of society, as represented by the teachers, may be at variance with the values and outlook of the people of the community whom the school serves. The decentralization of education in the United States tends to place the bulk of the power in the hands of the local community. An early instance of the sort of conflict that can arise from this kind of situation was the Scopes trial in Tennessee in 1925, where the community protested against the teaching of the Darwinian evolutionary hypothesis on the ground that it ran counter to a literal interpretation of Holy Scripture. During 1974 a community controversy in West Virginia developed over the use of certain textbooks which apparently fell short on the grounds of both patriotism and morality, according to the aroused parents. In fact, the ever-present likelihood of community censorship has led the National Council of Teachers of English to develop an organized resistance to attacks of this nature. In addition, ethnic groups within the United States sometimes exploit conflicts of this nature for their purposes. Jews have protested against reading the *Merchant of Venice* because of Shakespeare's portrayal of Shylock; blacks have caused the removal of *The Story of Little Black Sambo*, a children's book portraying a dark-skinned child with an inordinate love of pancakes.

Most recently among educational thinkers there has been a strong tendency to look at American society as moving in the direction of pluralism, from an ethnic point of view at least, and to assert that education within the schools must prepare the pupils to participate in this revamped social order. Naturally, with respect to the reading of literature, the emphasis is upon authors and selections which will reflect this function. In a sense, this was the moving force behind the article by Dathorne referred to earlier (1974).

It is very doubtful that many country educational systems are inclined to look with favor upon the notion that the schools should produce social critics and activists. Such a point of view is more likely to emerge in a country where the educational system is locally controlled rather than federalized. Moreover, it tends to reflect a uniquely Anglo-Saxon concept of democracy, which is not the only viable one by any means. Nevertheless, this glimpse of an educational philosophy, quite different from those prevailing elsewhere, and its implication for the choice of literature to be read in the schools is important by way of contrast if nothing else.

In a sense, then, for most countries in the world, we are at best at the concept of education as a mode of transmitting to succeeding generations the cultural heritage as it exists today, having been derived from the past. This might well serve as an initial guidepost to the kind of literature to be selected for study, in addition, of course, to the status or role of English within the country.

Still another matter of broad import remains to be considered. Much of the significant and valuable literature which has been produced over the past two centuries in England and the United States has carried a tone of protest. Some of it is the product of writers who are at odds with the society around them. A number of the novels of Charles Dickens were attacks on social abuses. Emerson and Thoreau, two of America's outstanding essayists, were highly critical of the contemporary scene. This was equally true of such American novelists as Frank Norris at the turn of the century, and of Sinclair Lewis, Theodore Dreiser, and Upton Sinclair in the twenties and thirties. Postwar England had its generation of angry young men.

In addition to social protest, many of our modern novelists and playwrights are preoccupied with the plight of the individual at odds with society. All this poses another issue. One must decide whether to include within the curriculum the first-rate work which may be considered to have dangerous incendiary qualities or to settle for second-rate expressions of contentment with the current scene. Naturally in countries that are unfavorably disposed toward the English-speaking world, especially England or America, literature in English may be selected for the express purpose of portraying consciously or revealing unconsciously the shortcomings of the society which it reflects.

The matters under discussion here are all considerations of a general nature, but they do serve to indicate the close relationship between a general educational goals of a society and the literature selected for study. There are, however, at least two principles for the selection of material which are immediately and directly applicable.

Certainly, at the inital stages of reading literature and for some time thereafter, the literature that is read should be contemporary, written in the modern idiom. There is little or nothing to be gained from subjecting the student to archaic forms of the language, obsolescent meanings of words, and subject matter that requires historical interpretation. Given the heavy current output of literature, the busy literary activity in all English-speaking countries, and the situation of having so much to choose from and so little that can be taught, it would seem to be self-defeating to include anything but contemporary literature—contemporary being understood as that literature which poses no linguistic difficulties for the pupil because of the time lag. This would defer Shakespeare to a fairly late point in the curriculum, the undergraduate university major, but it is questionable whether his work can be read with profit before this.

Throughout the course of this entire treatment, attention has constantly been drawn to the importance of the phrase "literature in English," signifying that literature is a product not merely of England and the United States but of a worldwide linguistic and intellectual commonwealth. For this very reason it would seem advisable to include literature written in as many of the English-speaking countries as possible, and until a point well advanced in specialized English studies, the literature of the various countries should not be presented in separate packages. Just as instruction in the English language is designed to open an avenue of communication with all English-speaking peoples, from Australia to Canada to the Caribbean, so the literary selections should provide the same kind of inclusive access. With these two principles of selection established, the contemporary and the worldwide, we may proceed to consider other factors that will influence the choice of literature to be taught in the English classroom, along with the questions of where it should begin and how it should be presented.

These questions must all be considered in terms of the role of the English language in the country generally, and in its educational system. Although the situation is somewhat complex, it may be best for our purposes to begin with those countries in which English has the role of a second language and where it is the medium of instruction in all or part of the educational system. In such countries, bilingualism is the goal of all or of a considerable part of the population. Generally there is a long period of school instruction in the English language, one which begins early. As a goal, we have established receptive acceptance of the culture of one or more of the English-speaking peoples. We must try to arrive at a coherent program in terms of these considerations.

For children at primary school level there could be an almost immediate introduction to literature, interpreting this term as language creation which is not utilitarian, language that is sheer fun, that at one and the same time feeds the interest in narrative and the concern for the miraculous. At the outset these various tastes and interests can be satisfied by nursery rhymes and by such stories as *Jack and the Beanstalk, Little Red Riding Hood, Goldilocks and the Three Bears*. With narratives such as the latter, there is the added advantage that there are no definitive versions or editions. Consequently they can be rewritten in whatever manner bests suits the background and linguistic development of the pupils. The overall purposes here are those of having fun with language and nurturing the imagination of the pupils.

At a slightly more advanced stage, the upper primary perhaps, some attention might be given to books and stories which were originally intended as, or have become, children's favorites. These include works like E. B. White's *Charlotte's Web*, Munro Leaf's *The Story of Ferdinand*, and more recently, Richard Bach's *Jonathan Livingston Seagull*. No matter what the official curriculum has decreed as to the vocabulary and structures which should be mastered at particular grade levels, these works should be presented without reference to them. There can be little doubt but that the story interest and general juvenile appeal will make for both comprehension and enjoyment.

At this point we come to the secondary school. Young people at that age, boys in particular, are notoriously uninterested in anything that smacks of culture or literature. They often can, however, be captivated by accounts of individual achievement. This points to biography or autobiography. Selections from such a book as Lindbergh's *We*, with its account of the first solo, nonstop transatlantic flight, if not the whole work, would have an instant and ready appeal. Possibly even better, because it is broken up into discrete chapters, would be a work such as Carlos Romulo's *I Walked with Heroes*. Another possibility, and one that would serve a cultural aim as well, is the use of folk material. The United States, for one, has a remarkable collection of frontier folk heroes—Davy Crockett, Paul Bunyan, Mike Fink, Johnny Appleseed, to mention only a few—and a wealth of story material about them. Again, since there is no canonical or definitive version of these, the language may be adjusted to suit the linguistic development of the learners. An important purpose in all this is to stimulate an interest in reading for its own sake, to demonstrate that school English is more than lessons in grammar and drill on vocabulary.

The senior high school would seem to be the proper time to introduce literature in the somewhat more narrowly conceived sense of belles lettres. Here it is desirable to begin with works that can be read in their entirety, if only to demonstrate that literary works do have a beginning, a middle, and an end, and that they do not all stretch out to infinity, to the despair of pupils. Short story fits in best with this aim, but with a little practice, the student can be trained to read drama at the rate of one act a day. At the final precollegiate stage some time could be devoted to poetry, poetry that is at once comprehensible and not esoteric in content. Much of Masefield, much of Frost will fit into this category.

Even a novel might be assigned at this point, modern but with a theme that is as universal as possible, one that is definitely thematic. Sinclair Lewis's *Arrowsmith*, dealing with the obstacles in the way of man's search for scientific truth, is an illustration of what I mean. All of this, of course, assumes that the ten years or so of English instruction have brought the student to a level where his performance in all four skills, and particularly in reading, does demonstrate reasonable competence.

For those who go on to college or university, the initial approach and structure should be in terms of literary genres, and the emphasis should be upon acquainting the student with the process of extracting the fullest meaning possible from specimens of each: the structure, the symbolism, the figurative language. At this point, also, one must begin to think of what the undergraduate major in English will need. The third year might well be devoted to the literature of the various English-speaking nations taken separately—or at least, England and the United States. For some of the other literatures, groupings could be made: Australia and New Zealand; the Caribbean countries, possibly combined with Africa. In addition, some rather more specialized courses, often comparative in nature, should be available: Dickens and Thackeray, the Eighteenth Century Novelists, Modern American Drama, certainly Shakespeare, Emerson and Thoreau, Whitman and Melville. Finally, in the fourth year of university work, a survey course should be provided, with strong emphasis upon literary and stylistic developments. Note that in this plan, the survey serves as a synthesis rather than as a scatter-gun introduction. This is not the conventional use of the survey, but it is one which has been successful almost everywhere that it has been tried.

Up to this point the major share of the attention has been given to what should be taught and when. Little has been said of the *how* of teaching literature. Now my answer must take on a very personal note. As a beginning, let us change the focus and speak instead of how the student is to learn. What I hope he would learn is how to be moved, powerfully moved some of the time, by what he reads. This can be induced only rarely, if at all, by lectures on the part of the teacher, especially if the lectures deal with what ought to move one, how one ought to react. Nor will it come about as a result of hours spent in word-for-word, line-by-line translation. Possibly the best path to the kind of reaction I am hoping for is an understanding of the meaning and the structure of the selection, in the fullest sense of the term. I am a strong advocate of the Socratic method whenever possible, at as many levels of instruction as possible, of as much class participation as possible. Again I cannot refrain from quoting what seems to me to be an ideal approach for the teacher of literature with respect to the work under consideration and the activities of the classroom: "Students are invited by some teachers to say how they as individuals respond to the work, what it says to them and about their lives; what it tells them about human beings and human life in general." I am well aware that my commitment to this emphasis upon *response* to literature may well be characterized as culturally conditioned and unsuitable in many situations. My reply to this would be that one never knowns how appropriate it may be until it is tried, and that I would prefer to err on the side of faith in the student rather than faith in a pattern of rigidly authoritarian education, which has had little in the way of positive results to commend it.

Thus far, I have said little in the course of this present discussion about the cultural component and how it can be dealt with in the classroom situation. Again, the topic scarcely lends itself to treatment on a formalistic basis; it is much better to take advantage of situations as they arise. Any consideration of the American folk heroes, the Mike Finks and the Paul Bunyans, provides the opportunity for explaining the prevalence of hyperbole, in concept as well as in language, on the American scene. The American commitment to a narrow literalism in its concept of truth, its approval of frankness rather than what it considers to be hypocrisy, its commitment to the work ethic, to excessive specialization, its concepts of the position of women and of youth; its refusal to recognize human tendencies toward venality and corruption—examples of all these are present in profusion in our literature. Not all are admirable, to be sure, but all are important to one's understanding of the United States. However, they must be seen in context, in action, to be understood, and so much the better if they are discovered or ferreted out by the student. They are not subjects for an organized lecture series.

In terms of what has been presented here, the curriculum and the place of literature in it are not too different where English is a second language from what they are where English is a native language. Indeed, the broad goals of education are much the same, namely a concern for stimulating and feeding a life of the intellect and for developing a humaneness and sensitivity beyond purely practical and vocational concerns.

Although certain aspects of literary education where English functions as a second language are not too different from what they are in native English-speaking countries, they also bear a relation to situations where English functions as a foreign language. These relationships can best be understood in terms of the differences between the operational patterns of the two kinds of educational systems.

To begin with, the aims of instruction in English as a foreign language are decidedly more modest than those associated with the English-as-a-second-language situation. We do not expect anything approaching an easy, or even a labored but adequate, bilingualism. In a sense, this will apply to the teacher as well as to the pupils. For the teachers we might well expect something like the command of the language described in the Modern Language Association's minimal standards for the preparation of modern-language teachers in the United States.

Since English is introduced at a later point in the curriculum and is the subject matter of just a single course, not a language of instruction, the total amount of classroom contact with and experience in using English is considerably less than when it is a second language.

Nevertheless, a fair number of countries in the foreign-language category provide four years of instruction in the secondary schools and a year or two in higher education. If this time were effectively used, and each year were planned to build sequentially on the preceding one, and in actual practice effectively did so, much could still be accomplished. In fact, this is the case in most of the Western European countries.

Yet, these very circumstances can only result in a later introduction of literature into the curriculum and leave less time to be devoted to it. Still, if the literature that is taught were well taught, it could provide a powerful stimulus to continued interest in the language, especially a language such as English with its incredibly rich literary production in so many countries of the world.

The reason for specifying a late introduction of literature in this situation is to avoid or guard against the use of literary texts as drill materials for the acquisition of language skills. Here I am in agreement with many modern language teachers in the United States who consider such a use of literature as totally inappropriate. In fact, even to try to give equal emphasis to language and literature within the same course often results in neither one being well taught.

On the basis of this it would seem wise to defer the introduction of literary studies until a fair degree of mastery of the language skills has been attained; it is particularly important that the student be able to read

smoothly and easily without constant thumbing of a glossary or dictionary. This will probably be in the fifth year of instruction in a well
planned and executed course of study; certainly no earlier than the
fourth.

Literature in the current or contemporary language is even more of a
desideratum here than in a second-language situation. Assuming that
one does begin to teach literature at this time, one must consider the age
of the pupil, the kind of interests he has, and weigh these factors heavily
in the selection of the literature. In general, fifteen or sixteen might be
assumed as the age of the fourth-year pupils in secondary school. What
will feed their interests? Undoubtedly material that is primarily narrative, where the story interest—what happens—outweighs everything else.
Again, short stories are probably the best beginning fare because they
can be completed in less time, giving the pupil a sense of achievement.
There is so much short narrative fiction that a listing would be super-
fluous. Much of the eminently suitable short story literature is to be
found in the better American periodicals.

But we must not limit ourselves to this genre. A travel account by an
Englishman or an American to the country in which the instruction is
taking place is likely not only to arouse interest, but in addition will be
culturally relevant in terms of what the voyager notices or does not
notice. It is also true that of all the varieties of poetry, the narrative is
generally understood the most easily. Finally, we should not overlook
the possibility of folk literature. The United States is rich in a particular
kind, much of which has been collected by Carl Carmer under the title
The Hurricane's Children (1944). This, of course, reflects the Anglo-
Saxon element in the country. The Indians had their own lore, some of
which found its way into a poem like *Hiawatha*, which had its source in
James Rowe Schoolcraft's *Algic Researches*. There is a modern collection
of Indian tales by Jaime de Angulo (1962).

As a second step one might proceed to material which derives its chief
interest not so much from what someone does but instead from the kind
of person he is, and from the interaction of character with character.
Hawthorne's story "The Great Stone Face" strikes me as an excellent
selection for a beginning here in that it presents several oversimplified
characters or stereotypes; the interest is in character but at a level not too
difficult for the pupil to grasp at that point. A careful selection of the vi-
gnettes in Edgar Lee Masters' *Spoon River Anthology* would be excellent, not only for their literary merit but for their cultural content as
well. As the last comment suggests, there is a place for poetry here—
Hardy, Frost, the Benets come to mind. And again the overall progres-

sion should be to move from that which is most direct in statement to that which is less so.

What has been suggested here should suffice fairly well to see the pupil through the secondary school. My emphasis has been on the principles of selection rather than on the pieces themselves. One could argue interminably over the comparative merits of Alfred Noyes' *The Highwayman* as against Coleridge's *The Ancient Mariner*. The crux of the question is whether or not the particular slot in the curriculum they are designed to fill calls for a narrative poem. And again my emphasis has been on the literary experience, upon response to the selections which have been studied. But let us be realistic. Not every student is going to throb and thrill to every selection he studies. If at some point in the course of every term he has this experience, even only once but hopefully two or three times, we shall have come a long way toward realizing what, according to my lights, are the aims of literary studies irrespective of the language in which they are conducted.

O. R. Dathorne trenchantly expresses the aim I have in mind when he writes: "By extending the frontiers of literature, we enlarge imaginative possibilities; we leave our old world forbears alone and in search for a new thrill of discovery, discard their static mold and regain a new focus of intensity, a novel turbulency of spirit" (p. 216). Somewhat earlier the *Northeast Conference Report* (Bird 1967, sec. 4.3.2) touched on the same subject. "When we speak of 'experiencing the work' we must distinguish between two extreme possibilities: an immediate reaction or response on the one hand, and something much deeper and more pervasive on the other. In the former case, we become acquainted with the work; in the latter we connect it in a vital way with our being; we assimilate it."

It is conceivable that at the first year of college or university level the student is ready for longer works, especially plays and novels. It is likely that my recommendations here will run counter to the most widely accepted practice. I would favor works which have been translated into the country's language. Moreover, and even more radically, I would recommend that the bulk of any long work be read in translation, but that the few really key chapters of a novel or scenes of a play be read in English and be carefully analyzed in class. For example, in a novel such as Sinclair Lewis's *Arrowsmith*, which I mentioned earlier, I suggest that the class read in English one chapter dealing with Arrowsmith's medical school education, especially in terms of Dr. Gottlieb's impact on him. I would select as a second chapter one of the episodes in his early career, where mundane obstacles stood in the way of his search for scientific truth. The most important chapter, of course, would be that relating his

discovery of the antitoxin. Then would follow the conflict he faced over
the administration of the serum, and the final chapter, where he regains
his freedom. I do not favor condensed summaries in English of the parts
which are not read; I want the student to sense the impact of the entire
work.

I would make much the same approach to the drama, although admittedly this is somewhat more difficult to achieve because the modern
three-act play does not break up so easily into small bits. But again, my
concern is not with detail. I readily concede that someone else might
select five chapters of *Arrowsmith* other than those I have marked for attention. If in his opinion they successfully present the gist of the narrative, the conflict, and the theme—well and good. Again, my focus is
upon principle.

As for the university degree candidate in English in an EFL country, I
would want him to have the experience of a survey course, again at the
conclusion rather than the beginning of his literary studies, and possibly
not the entire twelve hundred years of English literature. I would want
him also to have had the experience of studying one or two genres; the
development of at least one genre, or if not the development, certainly
the present state of the genre in its many ramifications. And finally, I
should like him to have the opportunity to study a single author for an
entire semester; Shakespeare, if you will, but there are certainly other
possibilities. Again the emphasis here is upon experience, upon a range
and variety of experience instead of the impossible task of knowing the
whole.

In our threefold classification of the role of the English language
within a country, English as a language of study occupies a central position. Its presence and use within a country is less pervasive than English
as a second language. Compared with English as a foreign language, it is
more utilitarian, more concerned with direct application. In effect, it applies really to a special group within what might otherwise be classified
as an EFL country, namely the scientists, the doctors, the engineers—in
short, to those fields of scientific and learned activity in which research
and new developments will probably not be translated into the native
language, and where authorities in the field are likely to come to the
country to aid in the development of one or another science or technology. In so doing, they will lecture in English, will assign books and articles written in English to be read, may conduct study groups or seminars in English, and may even ask for papers and reports in English. This
is the classic instance of English serving as "a window to the world."

To fulfill the needs and functions which have just been briefly sketched, all four language skills will be drawn upon, but reading will play a large role in comparison with the others. Even if the young professionals pursue their skills in an English-speaking country, the needs will be much the same. It must be recognized, however, that such a group within a country will by no means include everyone who is studying English. Moreover, the members of such a clientele will be separated out or identified fairly late, either by attendance at a special technical or scientific school or institute, or by enrollment in the scientific or other professional units of a university. Presumably, they will already have had some experience in English, but their special needs will justify a somewhat special treatment on a high intermediate or advanced level.

In terms of our interest throughout this monograph, we must ask what role, if any, literature has in meeting the language needs of such a group. In attempting to respond to this, I believe that we must interpret the term "literature" broadly, including within it what one might characterize as nonimaginative writing, particularly the essay, works that are written to inform rather than to provide the reader with an extension or a projection of imaginative experience. Prime examples from earlier writings would be such works as Gibbon's *Decline and Fall of the Roman Empire* or, on a more restricted scale, Huxley's essay "A Piece of Chalk." More recently, Charles Reich's *The Greening of America* would fall into the same category. In short, our concern here is with writings that employ the subject matter of one or another of the sciences or technologies, provocative in thought, but written for the intelligent layman and not for the specialist in a particular field. This is the kind of literature I would recommend as reading material for those whose interest in English is that of a language of study.

The question that this suggestion calls forth almost immediately is, why begin with scientific material written for the general reader, interested and intelligent though he may be? Why not introduce the student directly to technical works written in his particular field of specialization? There are a number of factors which must be considered here in attempting to arrive at an answer.

First of all, we must ask how narrowly or broadly the term "field of specialization" is to be interpreted, especially in view of the constantly growing number of cross-disciplinary fields and activities. Is a budding biophysicist to read only works in biophysics, or may he read in physics, in biology, or in both? Outside of the physical sciences, one might raise the same questions for the social psychologists or the ethnomusicologists. Certainly, in many countries or institutions, one could not organize classes for each of the special interest groups; there would be too many groups and too few students per group. What is even more important, perhaps, one could not find competent English instructors, capable of dealing with such highly technical and specialized subject matter. But capable English teachers should be able to deal with the kind of materials which have been described as being written for the intelligent layman.

On the basis of my own experience, I am convinced, moreover, that the technical terminology in scientific writing is by no means the major problem in developing a ready comprehension. Much more depends upon the position of modifying elements, and upon the words signifying logical relationships of sentence parts to each other—the conjunctive adverbs, for the most part. Mastery of these enables the reader to follow a logical presentation, irrespective of the particular field the writing represents. This is the kind of understanding one would hope to develop in the student's special field as well.

As a sample of the kind of writers contemplated here, one may mention Lewis Mumford in architecture and city planning, William Beebe in natural history, Buckminster Fuller on advanced technology, Charles Reich on ecology, Mary Hamilton on archaeology, James Harvey Robinson on psychology and human development, Arthur Schlesinger on politics and history, or Henry Steele Commager. Such journals as *Scientific American* or *Saturday Review* have frequent articles devoted to scientific subjects. Newspapers like the *New York Times* have staff science writers. Collections of readings for college freshmen in English-speaking countries, or at least in the United States, are often a good source of material. This is one place, perhaps, where entire works need not be read; single chapters may well have a unity about them. At the beginning of such a reading program, the selections should be short. I am inclined to think that they should not be simplified or abridged.

What might one expect the student to derive from such reading? First, a grasp of the main point or purpose of the selection. Second, he should be able to identify the assumptions or hypotheses upon which the writer bases his case. For example, a writer on ecology might accept the idea of population increase as a foregone conclusion, and because of this would expect an increase in energy requirements. Finally, the student should be able to evaluate the soundness of the logic by means of which the writer proceeds from his assumptions or premises to the conclusions he intends to reach. For the student, these are precisely the considerations that will matter, the critical stance he must be trained to take toward writings in his own field.

What should be done in class? Certainly only a minimum of translation from English to the native language. The little that is done on this score should be focused on passages posing special difficulties, either those which the students identify or the teacher suspects. It is only reasonable that the principal teaching activity be directed toward those very aspects of the reading which we expect the student to grasp: theme, underlying assumptions, logical progression, soundness of conclusion. Accordingly, class hours should be spent in discussion rather than recitation, in analysis rather than mere restatement of content.

The place within the curriculum of what has been broadly interpreted as literature will differ materially from its role in a second or foreign language situation. In a certain sense, it is being used primarily to improve the student's effectiveness as a reader, both in English and in his own language. So viewed, it could be called language-learning material. Moreover, we are almost wholly interested in the cognitive aspects of the writing and are very little concerned with the affective. Yet, in a very real sense, this approach combines an interest in literature with one in expressive effectiveness.

This concludes the examination of the place of literature in the curriculum when and where English is taught as a nonnative language. In our wholly justifiable concern with the language per se and with taking every possible advantage of the systematic study of language to facilitate the learning process, there is a danger of overlooking or undervaluing some of the uses to which language may be put, among them its function as a literary medium. The present work is an effort to correct what has at times seemed an imbalance, but in so doing to avoid advocacy for its own sake. It is hoped that the presentation here will be of some value not only for what the author hopes will be felt as a judicious appraisal of the potentials of literary study, but even more so as a thoughtful and even somewhat novel exploration of the educational scene and those aspects of it which have a particular bearing upon the place of literature in the language curriculum.

References

Angulo, Jaime de. *Indian Tales.* New York: Hill and Wang, 1962.

Applebee, Arthur N. *Tradition and Reform in the Teaching of English.* Urbana, Ill.: National Council of Teachers of English, 1974.

Bird, Thomas E., ed. "Foreign Languages: Reading, Literature, and Requirements." Reports of the Working Committees, Northeast Conference. New York: M.L.A. Materials Center, 1967.

Blatchford, Charles H. "ESOL and Literature: A Negative View." *Culture and Language Learning Newsletter* 1 (1972):1, 6, 7.

Brooks, Nelson. *Language and Language Learning: Theory and Practice.* New York: Harcourt, Brace & World, 1960.

Brownell, John A. *Japan's Second Language.* Champaign, Ill.: National Council of Teachers of English, 1967.

Croft, Edith F., and Kenneth Croft, eds. *Stories by Jack London.* Englewood Cliffs, N.J.: Prentice-Hall International, 1962.

"Curriculum Guide for Teachers." Mimeographed. Honolulu, Hawaii: Department of Education, 1974.

Carmer, Carl. *The Hurricane's Children.* New York: Willian Sloane Associates, 1944.

Dathorne, O. R. "Literary Studies in a Broader Context." In *Responding to New Realities,* edited by Gilbert A. Jarvis, pp. 189–227. The ACTFL Review of Foreign Language Education, vol. 5. Skokie, Ill.: National Textbook Co., 1974.

Ferguson, Charles A. "Linguistics Serves the People: Lessons of a Trip to China." *Items* [Social Science Research Council] 29 (1975):5–8.

Harrison, William. *English Language Policy Survey of Jordan: A Case Study in Language Planning.* Arlington, Va.: Center for Applied Linguistics, 1977.

Kintanar, Thelma. "The Role of Literature in Culture Learning." *Culture and Language Learning Newsletter* 1 (1972):1-5.

Kumida, Takaharu. "The Teaching of English in Japan." In *Final Report of the Regional Meeting of Experts on Teaching of English in Asia*, Annex 7, pp. 92-101. Tokyo: National Commission for UNESCO, 1971.

Lee, William R. "Editorial." *English Language Teaching* 25 (1970):1-2.

Parker, William R. "Where Do English Departments Come From?" *College English* 28 (1967):339-351.

"The Policy on Bilingual Education." *DEC Journal* [The Philippines] 2 (1974).

Postman, Neil, and Charles Weingartner. *Teaching as a Subversive Activity.* New York: Delacorte Press, 1969.

Strevens, Peter D. "Recent Developments in the Teaching of English." *The English Bulletin* 6 (1974):1-26.

Williams, Charles K., ed. *The Invisible Man*, by H. G. Wells. Simplified English Series. London: Longmans, 1959.

☧ Production Notes

This book was designed by Roger J. Eggers. Composition was done on the Unified Composing System by the design and production staff of The University Press of hawaii.

The text and display typeface is California.

Offset presswork and binding were done by Thomson-Shore, Inc. Text paper is Glatfelter P & S Offset, basis 55.

ISBN 0-8248-0606-9 $3.50

The Place of Literature in the Teaching of English as a Second or Foreign Language

In many countries the amount of time devoted to the study of foreign languages in the schools has not increased proportionately to the demands for heightened skill in their use. This has led to a reassessment of the aims of foreign language study and of curriculum content, but sharply divergent views have developed about the place of literature in such language courses.

Focusing on the English teaching situation in Asian countries, Professor Marckwardt explores the problem in a lucid, graceful, and engaging essay that illuminates some fundamental questions concerning the relationship of literature to the teaching of English as a second or foreign language. In doing so, he succinctly presents the fruits of his wide and long experience as a teacher and adviser of teachers.

ALBERT H. MARCKWARDT (1903–1975) was professor of English at the University of Michigan from 1946 to 1963 and professor of English and linguistics at Princeton University from 1963 to 1972. Among his many honors were terms as president of the American Dialect Society, the Linguistic Society of America, and the National Council of Teachers of English.

Of related interest:

English in Three Acts
by Richard A. Via

"A book which belongs in the personal library of every teacher of English to intermediate and adult students."
— **Christina B. Paulston**

"A Healthy classroom needs people who can be authentic. Students learning a language do tighten up and restrict the expressive flow of their true selves. How to release the energy is challenging. . . . Mr. Via has made a worthy contribution to a possible solution to the problem."
— *TESOL Newsletter*

"A delightful book, a joyful book which makes the reader feel pleased to be alive and an English teacher (if he isn't, he will want to be), and which imparts a lot of experimental courage and the confidence in Via to go with it."
— *TESOL Quarterly*

A CULTURE LEARNING INSTITUTE MONOGRAPH, EAST-WEST CENTER 天

ISBN 0-8248-0380-9, paper, $5.95

Cover design by Janet Heavenridge